1OOO YEARS OF THE OLYMPIC GAMES
TREASURES OF ANCIENT GREECE

TERENCE MEASHAM, ELISABETH SPATHARI AND PAUL DONNELLY

ORGANISED AND LENT BY THE HELLENIC MINISTRY OF CULTURE, ATHENS, AS A CONTRIBUTION TO THE CELEBRATION OF

THE SYDNEY 2000 OLYMPIC AND PARALYMPIC GAMES. DEVELOPED BY THE POWERHOUSE MUSEUM, SYDNEY

POWERHOUSE PUBLISHING

PART OF THE MUSEUM OF APPLIED ARTS AND SCIENCES

Co-produced by the Hellenic Ministry of Culture, Athens and the Powerhouse Museum, Sydney

First published 2000

Powerhouse Publishing, Sydney, Australia

Powerhouse Publishing

part of the Museum of Applied Arts and Sciences

PO Box K346 Haymarket NSW 1238 Australia

www.phm.gov.au

The Museum of Applied Arts and Sciences incorporates the Powerhouse Museum
and Sydney Observatory

Publishing manager: Julie Donaldson (Powerhouse Museum)

Editing: Rowena Lennox

Design: Colin Rowan (Powerhouse Museum) and Rhys Butler

Map: Rhys Butler

Photography: Georgio Fafalis (works provided by the Archaeological Museums of the Hellenic
Ministry of Culture); other photos as credited

Printing: National Capital Printing

National Library of Australia CIP

1000 years of the Olympic Games: treasures of ancient Greece

Bibliography

ISBN 1 86317 0790

Olympics — History. 2. Olympic games (Ancient). 3. Greece – Antiquities. 4. Greece – Civilizations.
I. Spathari, Elisabeth. II. Measham, Terence. III Donnelly, Paul. IV. Powerhouse Museum. V. Title:
Treasures of Ancient Greece. VI. Title: One thousand years of the Olympic Games.

796.48

Published in conjunction with the exhibition *1000 years of the Olympic Games: treasures of
ancient Greece* 19 July—15 November 2000 at the Powerhouse Museum, organised and lent
by the Hellenic Ministry of Culture as a contribution to the celebration of the Sydney 2000
Olympic and Paralympic Games.

Principal sponsor

Sponsor

CONTENTS

FOREWORDS

The exhibition *1000 years of the Olympic Games: treasures of ancient Greece* — the outcome of a laudable creative collaborative venture involving the Hellenic Ministry of Culture and the Powerhouse Museum, Sydney — is a major cultural event held in the host city for the International Olympic Games of 2000, the first Olympiad of the new, third millennium.

This juxtaposition of past and present is achieved through the display of an impressive collection of brilliant works of ancient Greek art, and seeks to present the values and characteristics that led to the formation of the Greek spirit of competition. The competitive spirit developed in the Panhellenic sanctuaries over the long course of Greek history and has been an object of admiration to generations down to the present day.

The Greek treasures that have travelled from their birthplace to distant Australia provide a broad public with the opportunity to understand an institution that first blossomed in the pleasant, welcoming valley of Olympia and was then consolidated in the other Panhellenic religious centres. That Panhellenic games were instituted in the major religious sanctuaries of ancient Greece reveals the close connection between the games and religion; it also points to the need felt by Greeks from all over the ancient world to gather together in one place, in full awareness of their ethnic unity. Through common sacrifices to their own gods, through common games, through participation in common festivals, which were invariably attended by a Sacred Truce, the free Greeks extended their spirit of competition to much higher spheres, fully comprehending its spiritual and intellectual profundity.

For ancient Greeks, competition was a symbol of their daily struggle, and rivalry provided an incentive for creation.

For the first time in human history physical training and competition became an integral part of social life and a major component of education: an education that considered the parallel, harmonious development of body and mind to be the supreme objective in the perfection of human life. The successful coupling of the two produced the good, noble youth, the ideal citizen who, through participation in communal affairs achieved what was best for the state.

The spirit of faith in mankind, in human brotherhood, in democratic equality and in world peace, which was born in the tranquil, harmonious landscape of Olympia, was foremost in the souls of the athletes who competed for glory alone, the only prize being a wreath of wild olive.

The mounting of this exhibition *1000 years of the Olympic Games* is for us an expression of honour to all those who share athletic ideals and the Olympic spirit, as expressed in the ancient Greek stadia, and to all those who still struggle for their ideals, and look upon victory for which the prize is merely a *kotinos* — a wreath of wild olive — as the supreme honour that will confer immortality upon them.

I would like to express my heartfelt thanks to all who have contributed towards the realisation of this exhibition, the purpose of which goes beyond the presentation of the ancient Olympic spirit, to promote, on a world level, cultural exchanges for the benefit of all.

Theodoros Pangalos
Minister for Culture of the Hellenic Republic

4

Australians are rightly proud that the eyes of the world will be on Sydney during the 2000 Olympic Games. The games themselves, however, will be only one focus of attention. High among the cultural attractions planned for the Olympics is this magnificent exhibition from the Hellenic Republic — *1000 years of the Olympic Games: treasures of ancient Greece.*

The exhibition is significant for many reasons. It includes objects of inestimable value and great beauty. Many of them have never before left Greece. The exhibition is the outcome of a unique collaboration between two Olympic host cities — Sydney and Athens — and a symbol of the enduring friendship between Greece and Australia. No two countries have a more intimate and long-standing connection to the spirit of the Olympic movement.

It is an honour for Sydney to be the custodian of these precious artefacts. The exhibition is Greece's official gift to the people of Sydney for the Olympic and Paralympic celebrations. It is a great and generous gift.

Greek culture is the foundation of European civilisation and therefore a deeply established part of Australia's heritage. Such exchanges give meaning to ideals Australians hold dear: the appreciation of great art, of civilised values, of democracy itself. In this spirit my government has publicly championed the restoration of the Parthenon marbles to their rightful home in Athens.

On behalf of the Government of New South Wales I express our warmest gratitude to the Greek Government for making possible this historic exhibition in Sydney.

Bob Carr, MP
Premier of New South Wales
Minister for the Arts
Minister for Citizenship

1000 years of the Olympic Games: treasures of ancient Greece presents the most significant collection of Greek antiquities from the Hellenic Republic ever to come to Australia, and I am proud that the Powerhouse Museum has the honour of presenting these treasures.

These ancient objects, the majority dating from the 8th century BC to the 3rd century AD, provide us with extraordinary insights into the contemporary Olympic Games as well as the ancient Olympics. While much has changed over the millennia since the first Olympiad — women are now competitors, and bull-leaping and chariot racing are no longer practised — many sports based on the ancient traditions continue in the Olympics to this day.

The exhibition presents these magnificent objects in a dramatic and interactive space — qualities for which the Powerhouse Museum is well known. Our thanks go to our principal sponsor, Intel Semiconductor Ltd, whose generous support has made possible the exhibition's cutting edge 'virtual reality' experiences including a 'tour' of ancient Olympia as it was about 200 BC, and a dedicated website that takes the exhibition beyond the museum to share this experience with the world. Our thanks also go to our sponsor Olympic Airways for the freight and passenger airfares between Greece and Australia.

The exhibition and commemorative publication are entirely due to the outstanding commitment of the many individuals and organisations who have supported this project over several years. Our thanks are due to the New South Wales State Government, the Hellenic Ministry of Culture, the First Greek–Australian Museum Foundation, the Sydney Organising Committee for the Olympic Games Olympic Arts Festivals, the Powerhouse Museum's former director Terence Measham AM, and finally to the dedicated staff of the Powerhouse Museum.

Dr Kevin Fewster
Director, Powerhouse Museum

ACKNOWLEDGMENTS

The First Greek–Australian Museum Foundation takes great pride in joining with the Powerhouse Museum to bring to Sydney for the first time these magnificent treasures of ancient Greece in celebration of the Sydney 2000 Olympic Games.

The Foundation's work on the project dates back to November 1996 with our first delegation to Greece for meetings with the Minister and Secretary General of the Hellenic Ministry of Culture. With the active support of the Secretary of the Ministry for the Arts, Evan Williams, and the then director of the Powerhouse Museum, Terence Measham AM, successive delegations were able to reach agreement with the Greek Government on the content of the exhibition. The triumphant news that Athens was to host the 2004 Olympic Games on the day the agreement for the exhibition was signed in Athens by Premier Bob Carr made that moment even more memorable than could ever have been imagined.

The First Greek–Australian Museum Foundation feels a deep sense of gratitude to the Premier for his guiding spirit, to Mr Measham for his energy and enthusiasm to see the exhibition bless this wonderful museum and to the new director, Dr Kevin Fewster, who has, in a relatively short time, brought his own dynamism to the exhibition's planning. Finally, the Foundation wishes to express its profound appreciation to the Ministry of Culture of the Hellenic Republic for its generosity in allowing the people of Sydney and their visitors to enjoy these wonderful artefacts that have never before left Greece's shores.

Professor Manuel James Aroney AM, OBE

Ταξιάρχης του Τάγματος Φοίνικος

Chairman

First Greek–Australian Museum Foundation

This exhibition and publication has been possible through the cooperation and effort of many individuals. The original concept for an exhibition was generated by the First Greek-Australian Museum Foundation with the support of the Honourable Bob Carr MP, Premier of NSW, and Mr Terence Measham AM, the then director of the Powerhouse Museum. This bold idea was graciously accepted by the Hellenic Ministry of Culture.

For assistance and guidance, sincere thanks are extended to the Hellenic Ministry of Culture staff — The Honourable Dr Theodoros Pangalos, Minister of Culture; Dr Lina Mendoni, Secretary General; Dr Lazaros Kolonas, Director-General of Antiquities; Dr Evangelos Kakavoyiannis, Director of Antiquities, Dr Liana Palarma, former Director of Antiquities; Nikoletta Valakou-Divari, Head of Archaeological Sites Division; Nastassa Papadopoulou, Head of Museums Division; and Smaragda Boutopoulou, Curator of Antiquities, Directorate of Prehistoric and Classical Antiquities.

Thanks go to the members of the First Greek-Australian Museum Foundation — Professor Manuel Aroney AM OBE, Emanuel J Comino OAM, Peter Cassimaty, Nicholas Pappas, Stan Halkeas, Dimitri Kepreotes, Joanne Alexander, Nick Malaxos, Paul Nicolaou, Tanny Tsanis, Stavroula Saunders, George Venardos, Nick Vlahadamis; and Professor J R Green, University of Sydney; Professor Alexander Cambitoglou, Curator Nicholson Museum, University of Sydney; Ross Burns, Ambassador, Australian Embassy, Athens; Dr Tiffany Urwin, University of Queensland; Dr Ann Moffatt, Australian National University; Ben Churcher, archaeologist, Sydney; Dr David Pritchard, Macquarie University; Stephen Curtis, exhibition design consultant; and Dr Robert Merillees, former ambassador, Australian Embassy, Athens.

Sponsorship has been generously provided by Intel Semiconductor Ltd and Olympic Airways.

I take this opportunity to acknowledge the many Powerhouse staff who have contributed to this project, in particular, Jennifer Sanders, Associate Director, Collections and Museum Services; Brad Baker, Exhibitions Manager; Paul Donnelly, exhibition curator; Susan McMunn, exhibition coordinator; Julie Donaldson, Manager, Powerhouse Publishing; Pat Boland AM, honorary numismatist; Dr Nicholas Hardwick; and Linda Sullivan, volunteer. I also wish to acknowledge the exhibition's virtual reality and website team: Timothy Hart, Chief Information Officer; Sarah Kenderdine, creative producer; Peter Murphy, digital photographer; Kate da Costa, archaeologist; Cliff Ogleby, Department of Geomatics, University of Melbourne; and John Ristevski, University of Melbourne.

Dr Kevin Fewster

Director, Powerhouse Museum

Hellenic Ministry of Culture

Committee of Honour

Theodoros Pangalos
Minister for Culture

Ioannis Beveratos
Ambassador of Greece to Australia

Dr Lina Mendoni
Secretary General

Rosa Ieremia
Consul General of Greece to Sydney

Dr Lazaros Kolonas
Director General of Antiquities

Dr Ioannis Touratsoglou
Director, National Archaeological Museum, and Numismatics Museum, Athens

Organising Committee

Dr Evangelos Kakavoyiannis
Director, Directorate of Prehistoric and Classical Antiquities

Elisabeth Spathari
Director, Fourth Ephorate of Prehistoric and Classical Antiquities, Nauplion

Xenia Arapoyanni
Director, Seventh Ephorate of Prehistoric and Classical Antiquities, Olympia

Dr Nikolaos Kaltsas
Head of Sculpture Collection, National Archaeological Museum, Athens

Nikoletta Valakou-Divari
Head of Archaeological Sites Division, Directorate of Prehistoric
and Classical Antiquities

Anastassia Papadopoulou
Head of Museums Division, Directorate of Prehistoric and Classical Antiquities

Smaragda Boutopoulou
Curator of Antiquities, Foreign Schools Division, Directorate of Prehistoric
and Classical Antiquities

Daphni Tsironi
Architect, Directorate of Prehistoric and Classical Antiquities

Artist's impression of the temple of Zeus at Olympia. At the right is the massive altar made from the ashes of animals sacrificed over years of rituals, which were mixed into a plaster with the water from the river Alpheios.

F Adler, R Borrmann, W Dorpfeld, F Graeber, P Graef. *Die Baudenkmaler von Olympia*, Verlag Adolf Hakkert, Amsterdam, 1996 facsimile of 1897 original, Tafel I, plate T CXXXII.

TIMELINE

Periods and events

About 3000–2000 BC	Early Minoan period (Crete)
About 3000–2000 BC	Early Mycenaean (or Early Helladic) period (Greece)
About 2000–1550 BC	Middle Minoan period (Crete)
About 2000–1550 BC	Middle Mycenaean (or Middle Helladic) period (Greece)
About 1550–1100 BC	Late Minoan period (Crete)
About 1550–1100 BC	Late Mycenaean (or Late Helladic) period (Greece)
About 1500 BC	Eruption of the volcano on the island of Santorini (Thera)
About 1200 BC	Destruction of Troy
About 1100–1025 BC	Dark Ages
About 1025–700 BC	Geometric period
About 1025–900 BC	Protogeometric style
About 900–700 BC	Geometric style
776 BC	First Panhellenic games held at Olympia (Olympic Games)
About 750 BC	Writing down of Homeric epics
About 720–600 BC	Orientalising period
About 700 BC	Black-figure technique at Corinth
About 660–480 BC	Archaic period
About 660 BC	Beginning of Monumental sculpture
About 620 BC	Beginning of Attic black-figure technique
About 610 BC	First coins invented in Lydia (western Turkey)
About 600 BC	Construction of the temple of Hera at Olympia
582 BC	First Panhellenic games held at Delphi (Pythian Games)
582–579 BC	First Panhellenic games held at Isthmia (Isthmian Games)
573 BC	First Panhellenic games held at Nemea (Nemean Games)
About 530 BC	Beginning of Attic red-figure technique
490 BC	Greek victory over the Persians at the Battle of Marathon
490–479 BC	Persian Wars
About 480–323 BC	Classical period
About 480 BC	Greek victory over the Persians at Salamis
About 456 BC	Temple of Zeus at Olympia finished (cult statue of Zeus completed before 431 BC)
447–432 BC	Building of the Parthenon, designed by Iktinos and Kallikrates with decoration by Pheidias
431–404 BC	Peloponnesian Wars, Athens against Sparta
395–386 BC	Corinthian War
338 BC	Defeat of Athens and Thebes by Philip II of Macedonia at battle at Chaironea
323–27 BC	Hellenistic period (begins on death of Alexander the Great)
146 BC	Rome annexed Greece and named it Achaia
80 BC	175th Olympic Games held in Rome to celebrate (prematurely) the defeat of Mithridates
AD 393 (or 426)	End of the Olympic Games
AD 6th century	Olympia destroyed in an earthquake and later covered by silt from floods

Personalities

8th century BC	Homer writes *The Iliad* and *The Odyssey*
612 BC	Sappho the poet is born
About 550 BC	Life of Pythagoras, mathematician
528 BC	Birth of Themistocles, Athenian democratic statesman (died 462 BC)
About 525 BC	Birth of Aeschylus, tragic poet (died 456 BC)
518 BC	Birth of Pindar, lyric poet famous for sporting odes (died 438 BC)
Late 6th century BC	Birth of Leonidas, king of Sparta (died 480 BC at Thermopylae)
450–400 BC	Life of Myron, sculptor
495 BC	Birth of Pericles, Athenian statesman (died 429 BC)
485 BC	Birth of Euripides, playwright (died 406 BC)
469 BC	Birth of Socrates, philosopher (executed 399 BC)
457–445 BC	Approximate birth of Aristophanes the comic poet (died 385 BC)
About 450 BC	Polykleitos, sculptor, active
429 BC	Birth of Plato, philosopher (died 347 BC)
384 BC	Birth of Aristotle, philosopher, later tutor to Alexander the Great (died 322)
356 BC	Birth of Alexander the Great of Macedonia, conqueror of the Persian empire and beyond (died 323 BC in Persia)
About 350 BC	Praxiteles, sculptor, active
About 330 BC	Lyssippos, sculptor, active
287 BC	Birth of Archimedes, mathematician and inventor (died 212 BC)
85 BC	Roman general, Sulla, used the treasures of Olympia, Epidauros and Delphi to fund the war against Mithridates of Pontos.
About AD 150	Pausanias wrote his *Description of Greece*

SIGNIFICANT SITES AND PLACES*

* This map features names of places relevant to the objects and essays in this book. Some places did not exist at the same time, and others are modern names showing where museums are situated.

MACEDONIA

•Amphipolis

•Pella
Thessaloniki•
•Vergina

Olynthos•

•Mount Olympus

Mount Athos

•Torone

EPIRUS

CORFU

•Dodone

THESSALY

•Thermoplylae

EUBOEA

PHOKIS

•Exarchos   •Chalkis

Thermon•   •Delphi   BOEOTIA   •Lefkandi

IONIAN ISLANDS   •Ritsona   •Eretria

ITHACA   •Thebes •Tanagra

•Oropos

Gulf of Corinth   ATTICA •Marathon

CORINTHIA   •Plataea

ELIS   •Perachora   Eleusis

•Elis   •Megara   •Athens

Corinth•   •Isthmia   Piraeus   •Brauron

Ionian Sea   Nemea• •Mycenae   Salamis

•Aegina   •Laurion

Olympia   ARCADIA   ARGOLID   •Epidauros   Sounion•

Argos• •Tiryns

Astros• •Nauplion

Tegea•   •Asine

•Bassae

LACONIA

MESSENIA

•Sparta

•Pylos

•Vapheio

ANTIKYTHERA

Mediterranean Sea

Koumasa

THEN AND NOW

Terence Measham, AM

The ancient Olympic Games began in 776 BC and ran for longer than a thousand years. They petered out during the rule of the Roman empire and as a consequence of the rise of the Christian religion, with which they were not compatible. Buildings in Olympia itself were converted for church use from about AD 400 but by that time Olympia was a ghost of its former self.

The traditionally accepted date for the origin of the games, 776 BC, has been established from a fascinating mixture of evidence. Information was first collected by the scholar Hippias who came from the district of Elis in which Olympia is situated. Hippias belonged to that intellectually glittering fifth century BC movement, the Sophists, who wandered through the ancient Greek world as probably the first ever professional teachers and helped to give Greek society its literally sophisticated texture. A century later, Aristotle improved on Hippias' information and it is the work of these two scholars that forms the basis of the historiography of the Olympic Games, including the listing of names of individual winners of specific events. As you would expect, archaeological finds also supply a wealth of information, particularly the clearly drawn pictures on Athenian pottery. Thus the objects in the Powerhouse Museum exhibition and this book, provide primary evidence of a centuries-long tradition that our modern Olympics attempt to emulate.

If 776 BC is the generally recognised date for the beginning of the formalised or codified Olympic Games, such events were well known on the mainland of Greece, among the Aegean islands and the coast of Asia Minor for a much longer period, perhaps another thousand years beforehand.

The region of Elis on the west coast of the Peloponnese was inhabited for a couple of millennia BC and Olympia emerged as a sacred site around 1000 BC. It was never a city. From an Australian perspective, it is tempting to see similarities between Canberra and Olympia. Both were virtually empty sites chosen for great things because they were politically neutral or, better still, innocent. The choice of Olympia as the site of the greatest series of athletic events in the history of humanity neither favoured nor gave advantage to any developed political or social entity.

But if an innocuous backwater near the west coast of the Peloponnese gave its name to the Olympics, it should be remembered that this great athletic tradition was by no means restricted to Olympia itself — athletic contests took place at centres throughout the Panhellenic world. The name Olympia is worth dwelling on because it holds the key to the most important condition of the ancient Games, one that distinguishes them radically from the modern series that began in 1896.

Olympia (and the Olympics) takes its name from Mount Olympus, which is well to the north and about a degree to the east of Olympia, on the border of Thessaly and Macedonia. Mount Olympus was the home of the gods, reigned over by the greatest god — Zeus. Long before the first games, Olympia was a rural shrine, devoted to the worship of Zeus. No one knows why Olympia should organise a racing event in 776 BC but it may well have been the introduction of a new concept, the notion of an athletic contest as a divine or sacred act. (The first meeting consisted only of a single running race and it was won, appropriately, by a local man, an Elean.)

The central and cardinally important fact here is that the Olympic Games were sacred and every aspect of them was of sacred significance. Nothing could be more different from our modern Olympics, which are entirely secular — no aspect of them is of any religious significance. Once this is understood, many other remarkable conditions of the ancient games begin to make sense, principal among which is their vital importance as a binding or cohesive factor essential to the texture and longevity of Hellenic culture.

Cross section of the temple of Zeus showing the colossal cult statue of gold and ivory that was over 12 metres high. It was made by Pheidias, the renowned Athenian sculptor, and finished before 431 BC.

F Adler, R Borrmann, W Dorpfeld, F Graeber, P Graef. Die Baudenkmaler von Olympia, Verlag Adolf Hakkert, Amsterdam, 1966 facsimile of 1897 original, Tafel I, plate T XI.

It is well known that the many different political entities that made up the ancient Greek world, city-states, lived in a state of tension and conflict. They were frequently at war with one another. But the sacred nature of the games was respected by all and it guaranteed immunity to enemies. While the games were on, a truce was on. The benefits of this to the survival of Hellenic culture are inestimable. The link between contest and immunity from war (I carefully avoid the word 'aggression') is reinforced by the fact that when that immunity, having lasted for a millennium, was no longer necessary, the games themselves lost meaning and impetus. Under the Romans and the famous Pax Romana, factional warfare was simply not possible and this was one of a few important conditions that brought about the demise of a very long tradition.

The connection between the ancient Olympic Games and military prowess is another element that distinguishes them sharply from the modern Olympics. Of course, nowadays, wars are increasingly fought via push-button computer technology. Missiles in the ancient Greek armoury had to be thrown by hand. Thus the connection between the javelin event in the ancient games and warfare is unmistakable. Even more obvious is hoplite racing: Greek foot soldiers raced wearing armour and carrying shields in one of the most popular contests in the games.

Chariot racing, an event that has not survived into the modern games, also resonated with military significance. In the Powerhouse exhibition, a magnificent Pentelic marble relief shows a chariot event, fearsomely dangerous, in which a helmeted, shield-carrying athlete clings on with his right arm outstretched to stabilise himself before he leaps clear of the vehicle and its left wheel (cat. no. 45).

It is clear from innumerable painted vases that armed combat was extensively practised in the gymnasia, the training centres for athletes. Athletic training in the ancient world was hard, disciplined and dedicated, as it is today. Unlike today, however, ancient Greek athletes were also schooled in philosophy and the meaning of life, which were considered inseparable from the training of the body. The gymnasium occupied a central role in society at large. It was a meeting place, an institution of prominence and significance in the community.

The ancient Olympics featured a number of close-contact events of the kind that are still popular today but were then considerably more savage. Boxers didn't wear gloves but taped up their wrists and hands with leather straps for some minimal protection. The marble profile of a boxer from Kerameikos Museum, Athens, shows his taped hand raised next to his head (cat. no. 43). The remarkable bronze arm from the Athens National Archaeological Museum affords a graphic illustration of a boxer's taped hand (cat. no. 41).

Wrestling was a major Greek sporting event that survives in the modern Olympics but nobody has yet dared to introduce the dreaded *pankration*. This was an all-in fight in which practically nothing was barred, although the judges, representing Zeus, frowned on biting. It was not unknown in these ferocious events for the winner to be declared posthumously.

Winning was all that mattered in the ancient Olympics. 'Winner takes all' is a phrase that certainly applies (cat. no. 56). Modern events have placings: silver for second place and bronze for third. The Greeks had no interest in or conception of prizes for anything other than winning. The only occasions when placings were recognised at all were equestrian events and then only when the same person owned all placed horses: first, second and third.

Modern events have records. We have watches; the Greeks didn't. But neither did they care whether an athlete won by a wide margin or edged in. It was all the same to them. All you had to do was win.

Nonetheless, there are clearly recognisable similarities between the ancient games and the modern Olympics. I have already mentioned the javelin but we have also copied the discus event. In the Powerhouse exhibition is part of a magnificent relief from the National Archaeological Museum of a discus thrower in Parian marble that shows a large sun-like discus framing the athlete's head (cat. no. 30). From Olympia itself the exhibition shows a bronze figurine of a discus thrower and a bronze discus (cat. nos 32 and 33).

The Greeks had several footrace events just as we do. They were run over different distances based on the length of the stadium. Though it sounds like stating the obvious, there was a starting line and a finishing line, just like today. It is still possible to go to Olympia and stand at the starting line just as thousands of sprinters did over a thousand years. The Greeks also mixed up five events together to produce the pentathlon, another of their ideas that we have copied.

One event that differed slightly from the modern version was the long jump. Greek jumpers carried weights (*halteres*) that were carved to provide a convenient grip, one in each hand. These weights were jettisoned at a critical point in the jump to achieve lift and momentum (cat. no. 34).

If a modern spectator was able to time-travel back to, let's say, the fifth century BC (to take everybody's favourite epoch) to the stadium at Olympia, he would notice a number of similarities between the games at Olympia and the Sydney 2000 games and he would also spot some differences. You will notice that I haven't used inclusive language, because in the main it would have to be a he! No married women were allowed in, though it seems that unmarried women may have been an exception. All participants however were male. Another startling difference that would astonish our time-traveller is that all the athletes were naked. And for that matter, all training was done in the nude, except for hoplites wearing plumed helmets, shields and greaves (or leg armour) up to the knee. Interestingly enough, it was the nudity of the Greek games that lead the tut-tutting Romans to put an end to them, among other reasons.

Today, no one knows why ancient Greek athletes trained and competed in the nude. There have been many scholarly and fanciful explanations, chief among which is that in some way nakedness equated with idealism or with the sacred. However, anyone familiar with the graphic art of ceramic decoration or bronze and marble sculptures from ancient Greece cannot escape the glaringly obvious conclusion that there was an enduring theme of homoeroticism throughout ancient Greek athletics and ancient Greek art.

In the matter of duration, the modern tradition has a long way to go before it catches up with that of the ancient Greeks — at least another 900 years! Even that wouldn't come close, in a sense, because the modern Olympics are staged once every four years. That is an interval, a periodicity, that was borrowed direct from Olympia, where the games were quadrennial. But in addition to the countless stadia across the Hellenic world, Olympia was the first and pre-eminent of four 'premier league' centres. The other three were Delphi, Nemea and Corinth. The Pythian Games at Delphi were also quadrennial; the Nemean Games were biennial and so were the Isthmian Games at Corinth. These major events were staggered so that there was at least one every year, and, as I have said, that went on without a break for centuries.

The great four were known as the *periodos*, or the circuit. And since the games were sacred, each of the four was ruled by a presiding deity. Apollo was the patron god of the Pythian Games, Corinth was devoted to Poseidon, and Zeus himself found time to look after Nemea. All aspects of the Olympic traditions were championed by patron deities. Thus Herakles, hero-cum-immortal, was the champion of training, of the gymnasia. A particularly fine statue of Herakles in Pentelic marble comes from the National Archaeological Museum in Athens to the Powerhouse exhibition (cat. no. 18).

Just as we have a cultural Olympiad today, so, in the original games, the Greeks took artistic events outside the stadium seriously. Women could participate in these events, and they did, with just as much competitive vigour as the male athletes on the inside. Whether it was wrestling, poetry or playing the lyre, for the Greeks, winning was all.

View of the stadium *(stadion)* at Olympia. Miraculously, the starting line with grooves cut for the toes to grip is still in place.

Photo Peter Murphy, Powerhouse Museum, 2000; © Hellenic Ministry of Culture

THE GREEK SPIRIT OF COMPETITION AND THE PANHELLENIC GAMES

Elisabeth Spathari

In the entire history of the ancient world, the Greeks alone may be described as an 'athletic people'. No other ancient people was so passionately fond of exercise and training, or had such a highly developed sense of competition. Repeated submission to the test, the insistence on improvement and striving to be the best were evident in ancient Greek military operations, formed the basis of education and culture, and were inherent in philosophy. Athletics were regarded by the ancient Greeks as an ideal of the highest order, relevant to religion and social life.

Homer's exhortation 'always to be best and superior to others' (*Iliad*, VI, 208), handed down from the elders to the young, was transformed into an ideal, the very essence of the training of the body and the mind in the ancient Greek world.

From the time of Homer, and even earlier in mythology, the ancient Greeks strove to attain some achievement, and developed their physical and intellectual powers to the highest possible degree, calling upon all their personal qualities to this end. The Greek myths, too, give prominence to the spirit of competition among the gods and heroes. Poseidon competed with Athena to become the patron deity of Athens. Atalanta was prepared to marry only the man who could defeat her in a race, Odysseus won Penelope's hand in marriage after a footrace and Pelops won Hippodameia through his victory in a chariot race.

The submission of oneself to the test, the spirit of rivalry and the endeavour to reach the supreme value of human being were even ranged against death through the holding of funeral games. The games symbolised life and hope, and the triumph of regeneration. The custom of honouring dead heroes with athletic contests is first attested in mythology, and was practised thereafter throughout the ancient world. Games were held at Thebes in honour of Oedipus after his death, at Troy for Patroklos, at Buprasion in Elis for Amarynkeus, and much later, in historical times for the heroes who died at Marathon,

at Plataea and at Leuctra. Alexander the Great honoured his dead friend Hephaistion by organising magnificent games in the heart of Asia, at Babylon, in which about 3000 athletes took part.

The spirit of competition was the initial impetus for the development of the intellect. The ancient Greeks believed that the creation of the whole human being demanded the development of both mind and body, and accordingly made athletic exercise part of their education. Through persistent training and exercise, they developed all their potential, in order to compete for and win the honour of victory. The athlete is one who competes for something, but it is certainly not the material value of the prize that attracts him. The most coveted prize in the Greek world was the wreath of wild olive, which was the only prize given at the Olympic Games. 'Pleasure is in the labour and the honour', wrote Pindar, for the Greeks competed for honour, not for material gain.

The Greeks were not the first to devise athletic games and exercises, though they were the first to convert them into athletic contests, in which the participants were fellow-competitors rather than opponents. Before the ancient Greeks, earlier peoples, in the eastern Mediterranean, such as the Egyptians in the third millennium BC and the Minoans of Crete in the second millennium BC, took delight in acrobatic feats.

The Minoan civilisation provides us with the earliest indications of contests and noble rivalry, while the true spirit of competition that was to lead to the principles and ideals of the Olympic Games emerged in the first great Greek civilisation of the Mycenaean-Achaeans. For these sturdy warriors contests were not the ritual acts they were for the Cretans. Their athletic spirit sprang from their military way of life and evolved in accordance with their own particular temperament. Though they borrowed acrobatic events from the Minoans, the contests in which they were primarily interested were boxing and wrestling, and they instituted two new competitions: the footrace and the chariot race. Despite the upheavals that took place in the Greek world during the so-called 'Dorian invasion', the Achaean view of athletics and sport not only persisted, but developed between the 11th and the 7th century BC, and it reached its culmination in the 6th and 5th centuries BC.

Homer was the first to describe the athletic contests of the Achaeans, and to indicate the importance of sport in their lives. The poet shows us a society that had developed a genuinely athletic spirit alongside its heroic ideals. Two kinds of contests are described in *The Iliad* (XXIII, 256–526) and *The Odyssey* (VIII, 97–253). In one of these, contests are held in honour of a dead hero and are thus funeral games, while in the other we see organised games. In *The Iliad*, any hero may take part in whatever contest he chooses, whereas in *The Odyssey*, athletes specialise in particular events. Homer's detailed accounts of games and the rich vocabulary connected with them are evidence of the existence of an athletic tradition. The word athleter (athlete) occurs for the first time in the text of the Odyssey. The use of these words was inherited later not only by the descendants of Homer's heroes, but also by modern Europeans, who made them part of their own language.

From the time of Homer on, rivalry ceased to involve hostile contest and became friendly competition. The character of the games in *The Odyssey* is the same as that of those held later in the Panhellenic sanctuaries. Participation in these games was not the exclusive prerogative of certain men, as in *The Iliad*; the athletes were specialists in one or more events, and members of an equal democratic society.

During the Geometric and Archaic periods (10th–7th century BC), the great era of colonisation and of the creation of the city-states, games started to be held in specific places and at regular intervals. The major Panhellenic games were instituted and held periodically, forging links of kinship between the city-states of mainland Greece and the islands, and the colonies that had been founded throughout the entire length of the Mediterranean coastline. The games united Greeks from everywhere who had common traditions, religion and language, and who formed a single entity, a people that was not confined within the bounds of a single

'Agon', the personification of the spirit of competition, represented as a winged divinity holding two wreaths.

Silver coin (Tetradrachm) of Peparethos, 500–480 BC, British Museum, London, from N Yalouris & al, *The Olympic Games*, Ekdokiti Athinon Ltd, Athens, 1976.

Scenes of wrestling, boxing and bullfighting.

Rhyton of Aghia Triadha, 1550 BC, Heraklion Archaeological Museum.
Drawing by K Eliakis from N Yalouris & al, *The Olympic Games*, Ekdokiti Athinon
Ltd, Athens, 1976.

Scene of wrestling from Homer's time; one of the oldest and most
beloved competitions.

Giant pyxis, 8th centuray BC, Argos Archaeological Museum, no. C109.

state. Virtually every year, these 'Panhellenes' gathered together at one of the great Panhellenic centres, where they had the opportunity to form an awareness of their shared ethnic identity, participating in sacrifices in honour of common gods, altogether at festivals and athletic contests. These gatherings were held at four sacred sites in mainland Greece, three of them in the Peloponnese (Olympia, Nemea and Isthmia near Corinth) and one in Phokis (Delphi). The usually high level to which the athletic ideal was elevated is expressed in these Panhellenic sanctuaries of the Archaic (7th–6th century BC) and the Classical (5th–4th centuries BC) periods.

The choice of these sites for the Panhellenic games was dictated by their geographical location, by the political evolution and standing either of the sanctuaries themselves or of the city that controlled them, and because games were instituted in these places in very early times in honour of some local hero or eminent deceased person, whose tomb in most cases formed the original kernel for the evolution of the Panhellenic sanctuary in question. At Olympia the games were initially held around the tomb of Pelops, while at Delphi they were associated with the vanquishing of chthonic forces (Pytho or the Python) by Apollo. At Nemea they were celebrated in honour of the dead infant Opheltes-Archemoros, and at Isthmia for the dead prince Palaimon-Melikertes. In other legends the foundation of the games is linked with the propitiation or purification of certain gods or heroes after an act of murder.

The cult of these dead heroes, linked with local contests, later gave way to the worship of an Olympian male god, Zeus at Olympia and Nemea, Poseidon at Isthmia and Apollo at Delphi. The games were instituted either by the god himself or by a hero-demigod who was directly associated with the main deity worshipped in the sanctuary, to whom the games were dedicated. This new Panhellenic spirit transformed these local games into newly organised united Panhellenic games, which began to be held in the major sanctuaries in the 6th century BC, though the Olympic Games started much earlier, in the 8th century BC.

At Delphi, for example, the first reorganisation of the Pythian games, which is attributed to the tyrant Kleisthenes of Sikyon, took place in 582 BC; that at Isthmia, by the Kypselids of Corinth, was in 582–570 BC, while the year

573 BC was considered to have seen the first celebration of the Panhellenic games at Nemea.

The development of the local games into Panhellenic festivals gave a great impulse to Greek athletics. Training and exercise, as they developed, became an inseparable part of education and culture, forming a dynamic element of the Greek civilisation. From the Gymnasia where the young men trained and were educated, sprang the ideal of the perfect citizen, of the 'good and fair' man prepared to defend the ideals of his tribe. The gymnasia were to dominate the political and social structure of the city-states throughout antiquity and remained intact, preserving the true spirit of competition even when the games started to decline.

The Panhellenic games reached their zenith during the 5th century BC. At this period athletics were directly related to the growth of democracy, and the games had a national significance. The victory of the Greeks in the Persian Wars (490–480 BC) was a victory won by free citizens, who were also trained athletes, against oriental despotism and effete barbarians. While the games were associated with life's struggles and the ideal of noble rivalry, the incentive for the athlete was always the victory and the fame that would accrue not only to himself, but also to his native city.

From their beginnings in the 8th century BC up to their abolition in the 4th century AD, the Panhellenic games were 'wreathed' games, an indication of the disinterested character that distinguished them from other contests. This meant that the prize for the victors was an olive wreath at Olympia, a laurel wreath at Delphi, a wreath of wild celery at Nemea and of pine at Isthmia.

The most important and brilliant of all the games were those held at Olympia: 'Just as, by day, there is not star in the sky hotter and more brilliant than the sun, so there is no more contest for us to hymn more glorious than that at Olympia' writes Pindar in his first Olympian Ode (Pindar, '1st Olympian Ode', lines 1–6).

The beginnings of the Olympic Games are lost in the depths of prehistory, amid the obscurity of a large number of legends. According to one of these, the founder of the games was the demigod and Dorian hero Herakles, son of Zeus and forebear of the founding father of the Eleans. Herakles was the first to institute a footrace and fix the length of the Olympic *stade* (600 Olympic feet or 192.27 m), and also the boundaries of the Altis, the sacred grove of Zeus. Another legend makes the founder of the games one of the Idaean Daktyloi called Herakles, who brought the sacred olive from the Hyperboreans, 'to be the finest point, the prize for the Olympic games' (Pindar, '3rd Olympian Ode', 15). In accordance with the most widely accepted myth, however, the games were founded by Pelops, the son of Tantalos, who came from Phrygia and defeated Oinomaos, king of Pisa, in a chariot race, receiving as his prize the kingdom and Oinomaos' daughter Hippodameia as his wife (Pindar, '1st Olympian Ode', 69ff.). This mythical chariot race was depicted by Pheidias in the 5th century BC on the east pediment of the temple of Zeus at Olympia.

From the mists of legends, cults and contests emerge into the light of historical times. After the so-called Dorian invasion and the collapse of the Mycenaean world, the Dorians of Elis displaced the Achaeans of Pisa as controllers of the sanctuary of Olympia, dedicating the site to the worship of Zeus, 'father of gods and men'. The games were held in honour of this god at least from the first known Olympiad, in 776 BC, when they were reorganised by Iphitos, the king of Elis. It was at this time, according to tradition, that the earlier chariot races, that is, the funeral games held around the tomb of Pelops, were replaced by a footrace over a *stade*. The cult of the hero continued to be observed throughout antiquity. The first Olympic victor was Koroibos of Elis.

In order to celebrate the Olympic Games and secure the safety of the athletes and spectators, three kings, Iphitos of Elis, Kleomenes of Pisa and Lykourgos of Sparta agreed to hold the games every four years, and instituted the Sacred Truce, which was essential to the development of the games. The Sacred Truce involved the cessation of all hostilities and was proclaimed through the whole of the Greek world of the time by special heralds, called *spondophoroi*, just before the games began. It originally lasted for one month, though this was later increased to three, while visitors travelled to Olympia. During the Sacred Truce, all wars between city-states came to a halt, sentences of death were suspended and armed men were forbidden from entering Elis.

Scene from the games given by Achilles in honour of Patroclus.
Dinos from Pharsala by Sophilos, 580–570 BC, National Archaeological Museum, Athens, no. 15499.

The Olympic Games were held at the end of every four years and had to coincide with the full moon of the eighth month of the year at Elis, thus falling in August. At first, they lasted only for a single day. As new events were added to the program, however, this was gradually increased to two days (680 BC), then three (632 BC), and from the 77th Olympiad (472 BC) the games lasted for five days. The Olympic Games were held for 1168 years, from their foundation in 776 BC until AD 393, when they were abolished by a decree of the Christian emperor Theodosios I. During this time there were 293 Olympiads.

Over the centuries, the Olympic Games were enriched with the addition of new events, which increased in number from the original single contest (the footrace) to 16 events. Although women never took part in the Olympic Games, there were women's events in the games at the other Panhellenic sanctuaries from the Hellenistic period through to the Roman times.

The organisation of the Olympic Games was the responsibility of the Eleans. The supreme officials of the games were the *Hellanodikai* (later called *agonothetai*), of whom there were originally two, a number later increased to ten in 348 BC.

They wielded great power and had many responsibilities. They could exclude athletes from a contest, and impose fines and punishments. The main offences leading to a fine or exclusion for an athlete were late arrival, refusal to obey orders, violation of the rules and bribery. The *Hellanodikai* had a reputation as impartial and incorruptible judges.

Two conditions had to be fulfilled before athletes were allowed to enter the Olympic Games: they had to be Greek, and they had to be free men, born of parents who were free citizens. As Greeks, they shared a common religion, customs and way of life, language and ideals. As free men they were members of a community, citizens of a city-state. Slaves, women and barbarians as well as those who violated the Sacred Truce, people under a curse and those guilty of sacrilege were excluded from the games. On the days the games were held, women, especially married women, were forbidden from entering the sacred grove, the Altis, on pain of death. The priestess of Demeter Chamene, a deity worshipped earlier on the site, was the only woman allowed to watch the games, seated on the goddess's altar in the stadium. The only known case of this prohibition being violated was by Kallipateira, daughter of Diagoras of Rhodes, who disguised herself as a trainer in order to watch her son and was forgiven since she was descended from three generations of Olympic victors.

The games were an expression of honour for Olympian Zeus and a kind of doxology. They were interwoven with the religious life of the ancient Greeks. The god, unseen, watched the display of physical vigour and athletic confrontation, and was pleased by the gathering together of so many in his sacred precinct. He it was who bestowed upon the victor the *kotinos*, the wreath of wild olive. According to Pindar, 'great glory forever attends him who has received thy brilliant prize' ('8th Olympian Ode', 106).

Statues of the victors and dedications by the faithful were erected to Zeus, father of the gods, in his sacred grove. The god also delighted in the cultural contests held at Olympia, with poetry, works of art, music and speeches, in accordance with the ancient Greek belief that the perfect man should have a sound mind in a sound body. The Olympic festivals were attended not only by sportslovers but also by philosophers such as Thales, Plato and Aristotle, historians such as Herodotus, and poets who wrote hymns for the victors, such as Bacchylides or Pindar, the poet of the Panhellenic games: 'and whoever is victorious has a clear golden sky, dripping with honey, for the rest of his life hereafter, thanks to the glory of the games' (Pindar, '1st Olympian Ode', 97ff.).

The brilliance and renown enjoyed by the Olympic Games transcended their cultural and athletic aspect and gave the Greeks, as they gathered together, a consciousness of their ethnic identity and superiority. Forgetting their life's needs, their human weaknesses and their differences, they recovered a sense of brotherly unity in the sanctuary at Olympia. Peace ruled the world and all were equal under the protection of the god. It was this spirit of reconciliation and peace, fostered at Olympia, that Baron Pierre de Coubertin sought to revive centuries later, when he founded the International Olympic Games in 1896. The revival of the Olympic ideals give people hope for a better life.

The Sanctuary of Olympia.

Plan by Debeyer, from *Olympism in antiquity* catalogue, International Olympic Committee, Lausanne, 1993.

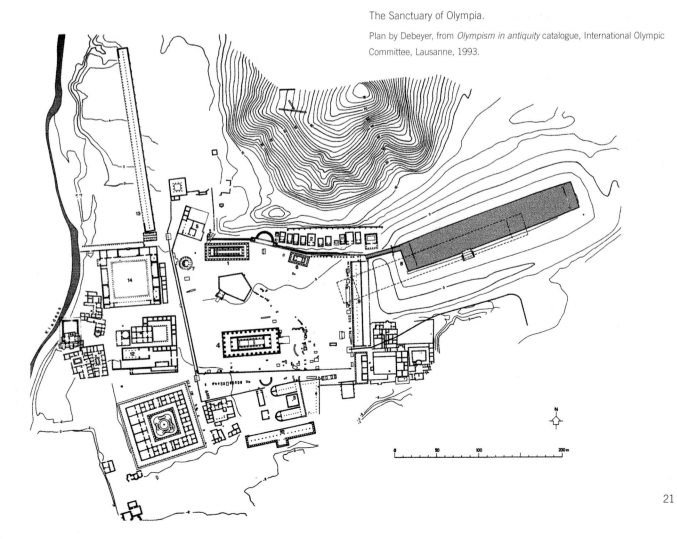

GRECIAN GRANDEUR AND THE WASTING OF OLD TIME
THE SURVIVAL OF GREEK ANTIQUITIES
Paul Donnelly

My Spirit is too weak — mortality

Weighs heavily on me like unwilling sleep,

And each imagined pinnacle and steep

Of godlike hardship, tells me I must die

Like a sick eagle looking at the sky.

Yet 'tis a gentle luxury to weep

That I have not the cloudy winds to keep

Fresh for the opening of the morning's eye.

Such dim-conceived glories of the brain

Bring round the heart an undescribable feud;

So do these wonders a most dizzy pain,

That mingles Grecian grandeur with the rude

Wasting of old Time — with a billowy main —

A sun — a shadow of a magnitude.

John Keats (1795–1821), 'On seeing the Elgin Marbles', about 1817[1]

When John Keats wrote 'On seeing the Elgin Marbles', educated Europeans were entranced with the surviving legacies of Greece's ancient and grand past. His emotive response to the sculptures taken from the Parthenon on the Acropolis in Athens by Lord Elgin reflected a general admiration. The discoveries of antiquarian treasure-seekers were filling private collections and museums, influencing the style and taste of that generation and those to come through revivalist architecture, art — and romantic poetry. From the mid 1700s these objects have been perceived as links to the origins of European culture and civilisation, another layer to the Roman remains familiar from the Renaissance, adding a tangible background to the ancient Greek poetry, myths and dramatic works that were already known and admired. These literary snippets of insight into the past were, and are still, being joined by newly discovered material, for who knows what else remains to be discovered? The Greek past still fascinates and remains topical — as shown by the current international controversy over the same Parthenon (Elgin) Marbles that inspired Keats' poem nearly 200 years ago.

The objects in this exhibition — sculpture, grave markers, votive offerings, ceramic vessels and sporting equipment — were fashioned over a period of 1500 years and come from a broad geographical area at one time or another within the Greek sphere or *koine*. Despite the diversity of styles, media and ages, a number of factors bind these objects together as a group: they all relate to the theme of sport, most have a religious rather than a secular significance, and they are rare and important examples of their kind. This essay explores the different ways in which these ancient objects have endured through time.

In the distant past, each vase and sculpture gracing this exhibition was a fresh addition to the products of human efforts already in existence under Greek skies. The pottery was removed still warm from the brimful kiln and its makers confirmed the success (or otherwise) of their efforts. The bronze was exposed new from its shattered mould, and the ringing of the sculptor's chisel on marble fell silent. But what has happened to these objects since then? What conditions have allowed this disparate group to endure? The variety of ways in which an object can continue to exist is always dependent upon the material from which it was made, and is often directly related to its original purpose and intended longevity. Organic materials such as wood, bone, ivory, leather and textile were undoubtedly common but only survive in exceptional circumstances. The loss of objects made from these materials skews the archaeological record, and dictates what is usually found and ultimately displayed — objects made from the hardy materials of stone, metal, clay and glass.

Despite the advantages of hardy materials, their survival is still sifted by time, and despite the inevitable and total loss of much material, there is a consistent activity allowing survival — that of burial. Burial was either deliberate or accidental: the former involved the conscious choice (as dictated by ritual or emergency) of ancient people, the latter relied upon circumstance. Counted among the deliberate burials are tomb gifts interred for the dead or votive offerings piously buried for the gods. And then there are the accidents — objects enduring, ironically, because of destruction through invasion, reuse, earthquake or even shipwreck. Such a cataclysmic event as an invasion or earthquake could have involved, for example, a sculpture, ceramic vessel or even discus being buried under a collapsed building, which, if the collapse was sudden enough, would have encapsulated the object with other potentially informative material. An ancient nightmare becomes in time an archaeologist's dream. Burial removed an object from a role in life that was ultimately destructive.

We are fortunate that throughout the past there has been a common human belief in some form of life after death and, concomitant with this, a belief that the deceased would benefit from the inclusion of gifts and personal belongings in the tomb. The result of deliberate burial is the survival of complete (if not always intact) objects of the kind most commonly seen in museum displays — their wholeness makes them easier to understand and generally appealing. In this way, objects from tombs differ greatly from the shattered fragments found in the controlled archaeological excavations of domestic and civic remains where, despite their relatively humble appearance, the object's relationship to other objects and features can be even more informative. The varieties of objects found in Greek tombs and graves vary from period to period but are represented mostly by pottery vessels and items of a more personal nature. In the exhibition this latter group includes jewellery such as the bronze and gold ring (cat. no. 1) from a tomb dating from around the 14th century BC, or strigils used for scraping the body clean (cat. nos 21 –23) dating from between the fifth to the second centuries BC. Despite the array of material obtained from tombs, it is a curious fact that, generally, as a society grew wealthier, fewer objects were buried with the dead. As one archaeologist has observed regarding burial goods, 'as societies develop, they become thriftier'.[2] This explains the lack of precious metals to be seen in this exhibition, with gold and silver most often remaining above ground — a social pattern Greek civil legislation in time entrenched by prohibiting funerary extravagance. Gold and silver metals remained in circulation (often literally in the case of coins) and were melted and recycled over time, while

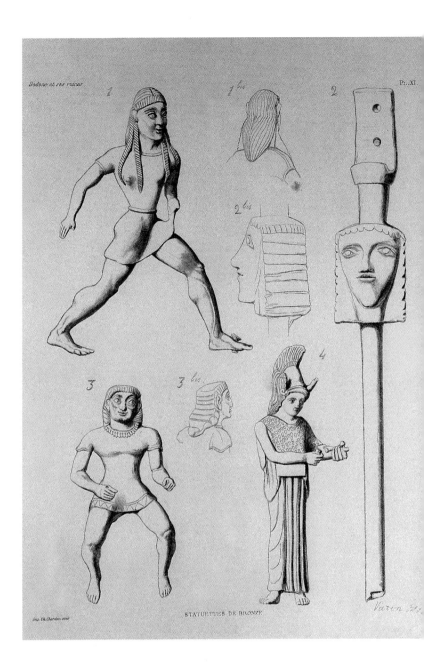

Plate from the 1878 publication of the excavations at Dodone, a sanctuary in northern Greece rich in dedications to Zeus. The female runner and horse rider seen here are featured in this book. Carapanos' presentation of this material demonstrates the use of publication in the development of modern archaeological practice.

Photo reproduced from Constantin Carapanos, *Dodone et ses ruines*, Librairie Hachette et Cie, Paris, 1878, pl XI.

TRESOR   CNIDIENS

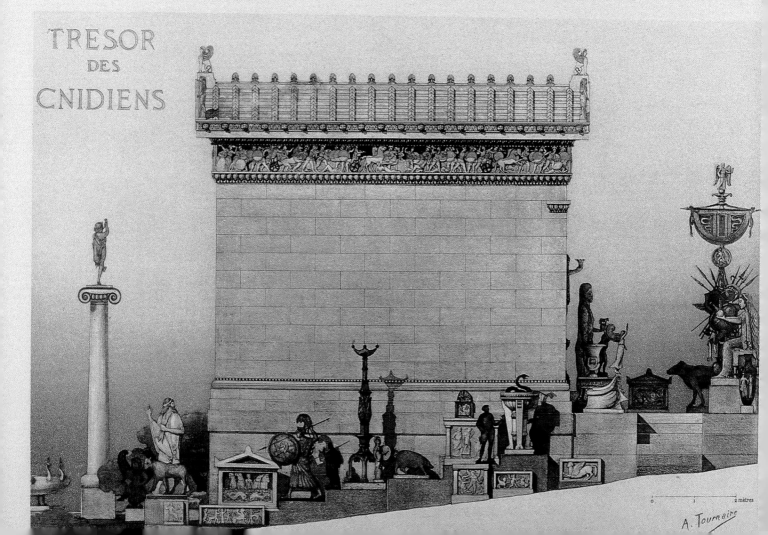

TRESOR
DES
CNIDIENS

A. Tournaire

more easily attainable (and relatively cheaper) materials such as clay and bronze were more frequently dedicated to accompany the deceased for eternity.[3]

The significance and frequent use of pottery as a grave offering can be seen by a cursory glance around the exhibition. Interestingly, it is probable that our appreciation of ancient painted ceramic vessels is greater than those who bought them, or even made them.[4] The greater instance of buried painted pottery instead of metal vessels, supplemented by information about prices in ancient times, suggests even large complicated vessels of the kind we see in this exhibition were relatively cheap. This is not necessarily a reflection of 'declining affection between kinsmen' and, in addition to laws forbidding extravagance, is possibly indicative of 'more spiritual conceptions of the soul and its future life'.[5] In the fifth century BC, when a sailor or stonemason might have earned 1 drachma a day, a painted vessel even larger than the red-figure amphoriskos (cat. no. 44) could cost under 3 drachmas.[6] Still, there is enough pottery that was mended with staples during ancient times to demonstrate their personal value to an owner. Other examples are the messages scratched on pottery, such as a piece inscribed: 'Kephisophon's kylix. If anyone breaks it, he will pay a drachma, as it was a gift from Xenylos.'[7] Inevitably our appreciation is increased — or at least changed — because of our distant perspective in time: we are fascinated by the painted scenes' ability to 'give us a more intimate look at the daily lives of the Greeks than any source, written or visual, ever before'.[8]

Much of the pottery in this exhibition depicts sporting activities that are otherwise rarely portrayed. Such sporting iconography might seem incongruous in the funerary context, but vessels depicting sport may have reflected the deceased's activities or aesthetic taste, and could have been utilised in daily life rather than being acquired specifically for funerary use. The

A reconstruction of the Knidian Treasury in the sanctuary of Pythian Apollo at Delphi, drawn by A Tournaire in the original publication of 1920. The treasury was a dedication in itself that held votive offerings given by the people of Knidos. Dedications were also placed around the exterior in a clutter very different from the stark ruins visible in Greece today.

Photo reproduced from M H Lacoste, *Foiulles de Delphes: tome II topographie et architecture*, E De Boccard (ed), Librarie Des Écoles Françaises D' Athènes et de Rome, Paris, 1920 pl. XI.

two panathenaic-style vessels (cat. nos 29 and 47) are a good case in point. Vases like these were made to contain the oil won as the prize in the Panathenaic Games (held every four years in Athens), and examples found in the graveyards of that city could have been won by the deceased during their lifetime. An alternative interpretation is the tendency of the grieving to represent the deceased favourably, a desire manifested in obtaining grave goods that represent an idealised, victorious and thus successful life. Appropriately, sporting competition has a long association with the dead. Originally, games were celebrations in honour of the deceased — a tradition mentioned in Homer's *Illiad*, which continued, for example, with the games Alexander the Great held at the end of the fourth century BC in honour of his dead friend Hephaistion. Vessels such as the bull-shaped offering vessel are less complicated to interpret as specific funerary gifts. Its function as a pourer of offerings and symbol of fertility is obviously sacred, as are the representations of the human figures on the horns performing the highly ritualised bull-leaping routine (cat. no. 2).

Deity worship in ancient Greece consisted in the main of sacrifices and gifts (or dedications) to the gods. An offering reflected the wealth and status of the devotee — be it an individual or a city-state — with the varieties of quality, scale and material we would expect to be representative of a diverse and socially stratified society. Animal sacrifice was an important communal ritual and could be one of the few times in a year when an individual ate meat. However, unlike the momentary act of sacrifice as a mark of devotion or prayer, votive dedications were a lasting testimony in honour of the chosen god or cult and this exhibition's appearance would be very different without these pious gifts.[9] In fact, a total of 16 of the objects in this exhibition were discovered in sanctuaries. These include a small bronze decorative element off a vessel from the sanctuary of Zeus at Dodone (cat. no. 49), bronze statuettes including a young girl (cat. no. 28) and a horse and rider (cat. no. 50) also from Dodone, and athletes from the Athenian Acropolis (cat. nos 26 and 31), as well as marble sculptural reliefs (cat. nos 54 and 56). The purpose of these offerings was to display gratitude for success, or to win the favour of the gods in the hope of their interceding on the devotee's behalf, in deliverance from sickness or other calamities. The religious

Head of Apollo from the west pediment of the temple of Zeus. The excellent state of preservation is due to the combination of earthquake and burial under the river Alpheios's silt.

Collection of the Olympia Museum. Photo Peter Murphy, Powerhouse Museum, 2000; © Hellenic Ministry of Culture

precincts or sanctuaries of Greek cities were enclosed open spaces encompassing altars, temples, treasuries and other buildings, and it is within the boundary of the sanctuary that dedications were made, displayed, stored and, fortunately for posterity, frequently buried.

Votive dedications were displayed or stored for a period as gifts to the gods, but just for how long undoubtedly depended on the value and quality of the dedication, as well as the social importance of the person making the dedication. While each state — even each cult — showed a great variety of religious practice, we are fortunate that one common practice seemed to be the deliberate burial of votive offerings that had reached their 'use by' date. The burial of votives on sacred ground in groups now referred to as 'votive deposits'[10] appears to have been a regular practice of disposal, in order to allow room for new offerings. It was a practical issue and the quantity of votive dedications that built up in a sanctuary can be visualised from a third century BC inscription from the sanctuary of Asklepeion at Rhodes: 'No one is permitted to request that an image be raised, or some other votive offering (*anathemata*) be set up in the lower part of the precinct … or in any spot where votive offerings might block the passage of visitors.'[11]

Though votive dedications were respectfully disposed of within the sanctuary, their often jumbled burial in what was effectively a pit in the ground betrays a lack of ceremony and their obsolescence. This contrasts with the careful placement and often complete condition of more fragile objects in tombs, buried as the primary and essential 'equipment' of the internment ritual. Votives didn't need to survive complete and relatively hardy metal artefacts fared better than pottery, which is generally less well preserved from sanctuaries.[12] Religious precincts are an extremely rich source of finds and votive deposits provide some of our most illuminating insights into Greek history — including specific events. The helmet of the victorious Athenian general Miltiades (about 550–489 BC) was dedicated to Zeus at Olympia along with spoils of war such as weapons, insignia standards and armour (booty was a popular dedication of thanks for victory) after the Athenian victory over the Persians at Marathon in 490 BC. Its battered surface and narrow eye slits were present at the battle that was to lead to Athens' political and artistic supremacy, and change irrevocably the course of Greek history.

The form of a votive is often both indicative of and appropriate to the reason for its dedication. Since sport was in honour of the gods and victory was gained by their grace, sporting dedications were numerous. It is not surprising that 'in short, the sanctuary became a marvellous monumental host of dynamic athletes — and dynamic art'.[13] The bronze head of a statuette from the Athenian Acropolis (cat. no. 16) was probably dedicated to Athena in thanks for a sporting victory (indicated by the fillet around the head, in reality a woollen ribbon worn in victory), as were other examples, such as the marble dedicatory relief from Sounion of a youth crowning himself (cat. no. 56). An inscribed relief of a victorious athlete captures the danger of the *apobates* (cat. no. 45), whose role it was to leap off and on the speeding chariot. This is an idealised representation of the *apobates* (for only after three wins could an athlete be honoured with a realistic likeness) a moment before the leap. Other gifts to the gods are just as informative, if less dramatic. The bronze figurine of a discus thrower (cat. no. 32) from Olympia is inscribed 'I belong to Zeus', showing its votive purpose to the supreme deity of Olympia, the god in whose honour the games were held. A votive figurine from the Acropolis is engraved 'Sacred to Athena; Phialos [dedicated me as] a tithe'. Were these devoted in anticipation of victory or in thanks after the event? Was Phialos a winner in the Panathenaic Games or a hopeful entrant? A few objects, such as the bronze votive discus from Olympia dedicated by the winner of the AD 241 pentathlon, Publius Asklepiades (cat. no. 10), are more informative. With its inscription on both sides, it is a valuable historical document in its own right, capable of providing new information and corroborating other written sources regarding events, participants and the origins of the games.

In addition to small portable votives of the kind most likely to be buried in deposits, large-scale sculpture and sculptural groups were also popular and more prestigious offerings, but their survival is less common. Temple precincts in ancient times would have resembled open-air art galleries or museums (see image p 24), and it was quite possible that large-scale material was displayed for several centuries. The prominence of such items made them easy targets for looters during times of war and political instability. Metal — gold, silver and bronze statues — could be readily melted down for reuse as new artworks, as well as weapons and bullion.

Ironically stone and clay objects fared better in violent situations, where their survival — albeit in fragments — was possible. Much of the sculpture of the pediments from the temple of Zeus at Olympia have been reconstructed from fragments that survived the temple's gradual desecration along with other 'pagan' sanctuaries, probably from as early as the reign of Constantine (AD 306–337). Whatever survived later toppled to the ground in an earthquake of the sixth century AD, where it became covered by the protective river silt and eroding soil of adjacent Mount Kronos (see image p 26). Around the AD 420s, during the reign of Theodosius II (AD 408–450), the huge (12.5 m) gold and ivory cult statue of Zeus was removed to Constantinople. It had been a focus of worship in Olympia for 800 years, one of the seven wonders of the ancient world, a vision that seemed in 167 BC for the otherwise hard-to-impress Roman general, Lucius Aemilius Paullus, 'Jove's very incarnation'. On the pattern of survival so far described, a gold and ivory monumental sculpture was doomed to disappear. Once it was in Constantinople it was the focal point of a gallery in the private collection of Lausus, where it possibly inspired the now commonplace bearded face of Christ.[14] In around AD 475 it was destroyed in a fire that consumed the palace in which the statue was placed. Its ivory 'flesh' and wooden frame would have been consumed — its golden robes had disappeared when ignominiously looted probably over a century earlier.

In Athens, a rare combination of violence and deliberate burial ensured the unusually complete survival of many large statues from the Acropolis. These statues have contributed to the modern understanding of that city's sculptural development. Caches of *kouroi* and *korai* (young male and female) dedicatory sculptures had been, as Nigel Spivey writes, 'piously interred' by the Athenians after the Persian sacking of their city and the desecration of their sanctuaries in 480 BC.[15] The statues were deposited before the erection, in the last half of the fifth century BC, of the buildings on the Acropolis today. Religious practice of course

continued, and new votive dedications, including the statuette of an athlete of which the head remains (cat. no. 16), replaced those ruined in the invasion. The pattern of deliberate burial in the disposal of these votives, although stimulated by invasion and destruction, was consistent with the pious and respectful treatment of smaller dedications buried as part of the 'housekeeping' activities within the sanctuary.

Some objects survive through burial, some through reuse. The reuse of metals involved the complete melting of the bronze, silver or gold, and consequent annihilation of its original form. Large-scale bronze sculpture was particularly vulnerable and if it did survive, which it rarely did, it is usually through accident — especially shipwreck, the calamity that saved the only piece in this exhibition from a larger-than-life-size bronze statue. It is the arm of a boxer from the Antikythera wreck (cat. no. 41), discovered by fishermen in 1900 and dating from around the second century BC. The importance and rarity of these large bronzes, which survive firstly because of accident (subsequent to looting, which is probably why they were on the ships in the first place), and secondly because of accidental discovery, makes them icons of original Greek statuary. The larger-than-life-size bronze god, now thought to be Zeus, found in the wreck site off Cape Artemision, and the charioteer from Delphi (*left* and *right*), a survivor thanks to landslide, are exceptional examples among a relative multitude of informative but nevertheless derivative Roman marble copies of Greek bronze originals.

Significantly, stone sculpture was more likely to survive than metal, a generalisation confirmed by this exhibition. There are the inevitable exceptions to the apparent invincibility of stone, including the deliberate burning of marble to make lime for mortar. Though not as totally destructive as burning, the intentional defacement by early Christian and Muslim iconoclasts of sculptures and reliefs featuring humans and animals was stimulated by superstition.

The reuse of material makes perfect economic sense, saving as it does the time and labour of sourcing materials and the expense of processing. Stone was sought after and frequently 'robbed' from ancient sites and incorporated into newer structures. This can be useful for archaeologists, but the best protection against dismantling for any building was constant use, and a good case in point is the Parthenon on the Acropolis in Athens. After the adoption of Christianity in Greece, the Parthenon was converted into an Orthodox church in the fifth century AD. It was at this time that the sculptural metopes were defaced as inappropriate symbols for its new role.[16] Little changed while it was the Catholic cathedral of Athens in the 1200s, and a minaret was added in the 1400s during the Ottoman occupation of Greece. For over 2000 years the Parthenon survived mostly intact, until a Venetian shell scored a direct hit on the temple in 1687, while it was being used as a Turkish gunpowder store. The damage was extensive and restoration continues today. In contrast to the Parthenon, the usual fate of buildings was disuse and eventual ruin, after which they became convenient 'quarries' of ready-cut and finished blocks of stone. Such behavior wasn't irreverent, but practical and, on occasion, mystical. Until relatively modern times antiquities were believed to have been invested with supernatural qualities and could be incorporated in a dwelling — usually over the front door — to allow the occupants to benefit from the fragments' protective qualities thought to have accrued from the mists of time.[17]

In times of emergency, reappropriation could even occur quite soon after an object had been made, and this is shown by at least three examples in the exhibition. Two were reused within the defensive walls hastily reconstructed from 479 BC around Athens, which was otherwise vulnerable to attack (mainly from the rival Greek city of Sparta) after the walls' destruction by the Persians. The historian Thucydides (around 455–400 BC) comments:

> *I.89.3 The Athenian people, when the barbarians [Persians] had left their country, immediately started bringing back their children and wives and their remaining property from the places to which they had removed them for safety, and prepared to rebuild their city and walls; for only small sections of their surrounding wall were still standing and most of their houses were in ruins... Meanwhile the entire population of the city should build the wall, sparing neither private nor public buildings which might be of some use in the work, but demolishing everything... I.93.1 In this way the Athenians fortified their city in a short time.[18]*

The grave marker (stele) depicting a boxer (cat. no. 43) and the relief funerary base (cat. no. 24) were built into the

The charioteer coming to light on the day of its discovery, 28 April 1896.
Reproduced from Francois Chamoux, *Foiulles de Delphes: tome IV fascicule 5, monuments figures — sculpture*, E De Boccard (ed), Ouvrage publié avec concours du Centre National de la Recherch Scientifique, Paris, 1955, pl. II.

(Left) Charioteer from Delphi, an offering by Polyzalus in thanks for victory in the Pythian (Delphi) Games held in 478 or 474 BC. It survives (with a few fragments of its chariot and horses) because of a landslide — a common occurrence in the steep landscape of Delphi.
Collection of Delphi Archaeological Museum. Photo reproduced from M Theophile Homolle, *Foiulles de Delphes: tome IV fascicule I, monuments figures — sculpture*, Fontemoing & Cie. (eds), Librarie Des Écoles Françaises D' Athènes et de Rome, Paris, 1905, pl. XLIX, © Hellenic Ministry of Culture.

Themistoclean Walls (named after Themistocles (about 523 – about 458 BC), the Athenian general and statesman who lobbied for their construction), which by the middle of the fifth century BC connected Athens with its port Piraeus. The boxer stele was about 70 years old by the time it was smashed — either in the Persian invasion or during the construction of the walls through the Kerameikos cemetery in which the stele would have stood tall as a memorial. Whatever the initial cause of its destruction, it is significant that in the process of turning it into a convenient block with which to build, the fragment may have been trimmed sensitively, with respect for the handsome profile. Similar treatment given to the grave stele of a discus thrower (cat. no. 30) suggests a pattern akin to the respectful disposal of votive dedications already discussed. Such treatment would have depended on the sensitivity of individuals rather than on official policy, which was, Thucydides suggested, one of extreme swiftness:

> *I.93.2 Even today [about 420 BC] it is clear that the building took place in a hurry; for the foundations are laid on all sorts of stone and these were not shaped so as to fit together but each was laid just as it were brought forward, and many stelai from tombs and pieces of sculpture were built into the wall. For the boundaries of the city were extended on all sides, and because of this, they used everything they could find in their haste.*[19]

The relief funerary base (cat. no. 24) was already a convenient block for building into the Themistoclean Walls and had been made only around 30 years before it was assigned its new role.

After the Themistoclean Walls were built, other defensive walls were made to protect Athens, often proving to be 'a godsend to the archaeologist, a veritable museum of the earlier glories of the city'.[20] From the later wall built in around AD 250 under the Roman emperor Valerian comes the base of a commemorative monument (cat. no. 46). It was made in the early fourth century BC and its worn appearance attests to its probable exposure to the elements for some centuries until its incorporation into the wall 650 years later. The Athenians commemorated in these monuments contributed to their city's welfare long after their death.

Keats' emotive response to the 'Grecian grandeur' of the Parthenon sculptures has been reflected in writing about Greek antiquities for the past two centuries. Keats was moved and inspired by the sculpture he and others flocked to see in London. Beyond this ultimately romantic approach, modern art historians, classicists and archaeologists seek to interpret the same objects as social, economic, technological and artistic examples of long-past ways of life. All the objects in this exhibition admirably serve such purposes, but it is hard not to empathise with Keats' sensitive vision and celebrate their long and eventful journeys of survival in the temporal lottery that history — not so indiscriminately — apportions.

Endnotes

1   John Keats, *The complete poems*, 3rd edn, ed John Barnard, Penguin, London, 1988.

2   B A Sparkes, *The red and the black*, Routledge, London, 1996, p 146, from an observation made by V G Childe, *Progress and archaeology*, Watts, London, 1944, pp 86–7.

3   Most examples of silver and gold vessels, and particularly coins, have been found as hoards hurriedly buried in times of emergency, such as invasion, and never recovered by the owner.

4   Sparkes, *The red and the black*, pp 140–5.

5   Childe, *Progress and archaeology*, p 88.

6   Sparkes, *The red and the black*, p 143.

7   M Elston, 'Ancient repairs of Greek vases in the J Paul Getty Museum', in *The J Paul Getty Museum Journal*, 18, 1990, and B A Sparkes, *Greek pottery: an introduction*, Manchester University Press, Manchester, 1991, p 63.

8   H A Shapiro, *Art, myth and culture: Greek vases from Southern collections*, New Orleans Museum of Art in conjunction with Tulane University, New Orleans, 1989, p 10.

9   Some examples of votive dedications combine both sacrifice and gift by 'freezing' the moment and incorporating a representation of a sacrificial animal. The most famous example is the marble *kouros* statue named as *Moscophoros* (calf bearer) for the calf wrapped around the figure's shoulders on an eternal journey to the altar.

10 R M Cook, *Greek painted pottery*, Methuen & Co, London, 1960, p 370.

11 Nigel Spivey, *Understanding Greek sculpture*, Thames and Hudson, London, 1996, p 83.

12 Arthur Lane, *Greek pottery*, Faber & Faber, London, 1947, p 8. Also, the Kabeiron in Boeotia is a site famous for its bronze votive deposits dedicated to the Kabeiroi, the deities of the Boeotian mystery cult.

13 Nigel Spivey, *Understanding Greek sculpture*, p 104.

14 C Mango, M Vickers and E D Francis, 'The palace of Lausus at Constantinople and its collection of ancient statues', *Journal of the history of collections*, 4(1), 1992, p 95.

15 Nigel Spivey, *Understanding Greek sculpture*, p 138.

16 B F Cook, *The Elgin Marbles*, 2nd edn, British Museum Press, London, 1997, p 20.

17 Yannis Hamilakis, 'Stories from exile: fragments from the cultural biography of the Parthenon (or 'Elgin') marbles', *World archaeology*, 31(2), 1999, pp 303–20.

18 Thucydides, quoted in M Dillon and L Garland, *Ancient Greece: social and historical documents from Archaic times to the death of Socrates*, Routledge, London, 1994, p 217.

19 Thucydides, quoted in M Dillon and L Garland, *Ancient Greece: social and historical documents from Archaic times to the death of Socrates*, p 218.

20 R E Wycherley, *The stones of Athens*, Princeton University Press, Princeton, 1978, p 23.

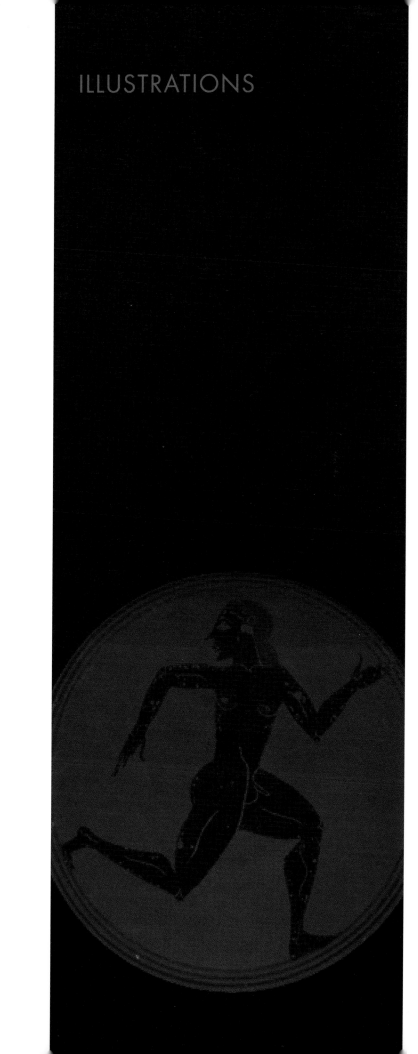

ILLUSTRATIONS

ORIGINS

Some of the earliest recorded sporting games occurred around the Aegean Sea at the end of the Middle Bronze Age (around 1600 BC), long before the Olympic Games, which are traditionally said to have started in 776 BC. Homer's *Iliad*, written in the 8th century BC, is set in the Bronze Age. It tells of the funerary games organised by the mythical hero Achilles for Patroklos, his friend killed in the Trojan War around 1200 BC. About 600 years after Homer wrote the *Iliad* Alexander the Great, during his military campaigns, mourned the death of Hephaistion with extravagant funerary games in 324 BC. As well as their funerary and, therefore, religious significance, these games also reflected heroism and strength required in battle.

The objects in this section illustrate some of the earliest sports recorded. The dangerous practice of bull-leaping originated in Crete around 2000 BC. Representations of this spectacular and ritualistic event appear in Minoan (Cretan) style wall frescoes not just in Crete, but also the Nile Delta in Egypt.

The concept of the chariot had been imported from Western Asia and for the Mycenaean Greeks, whose influence ranged all over the Mediterranean, racing must have seemed a logical development of war, transport and hunting.

Paul Donnelly

SIGNET RING

Cat no. 1
Provenance: Asine, chamber tomb I
Late Helladic IIB–IIIA (15th–14th century BC)
Gold and bronze
1.8 (h) x 2.8 (w) cm
National Archaeological Museum, Athens, 10275

Bull-leaping is a dominant motif in the Creto-Mycenaean artistic repertoire and is depicted in wall-paintings and on signet rings, seal stones and potsherds in the Pictorial style, and on the terracotta sarcophagus from Tanagra. On this bronze finger ring with an oval bezel, part of the gold sheathing is preserved. On it is an intaglio scene of a bull-leaper wearing a Minoan loincloth and executing a spectacular leap over a galloping bull. The presence of the bull-leaping contest motif on Middle Minoan III seals attests to its Minoan origins. The event is depicted spectacularly in the bull-leaping fresco from the palace at Knossos.

Maria Vlassopoulou-Karydi

Bibliography:
O Frödin and A Persson. *Asine*, 1938, 372, fig. 241.
A Sakellariou. *CMS I*, 1964, 224, no. 200.
A Sakellariou. *Μυκηναϊκή Σφραγιδογλυφία*, Athens, 1966, 58.

BULL RHYTON

Cat no. 2

Provenance: Koumasa

Early Minoan II – Middle Minoan II (2500–1900 BC)

Clay

15 (h, with handle) x 20.5 (l) cm

Heraklion Archaeological Museum, Crete, 4126

Bull-leaping was a contest involving bulls in which young men and women took part, probably to the accompaniment of musical instruments. It has been suggested that the events took place during fertility rituals, though according to Reichel, they were held in honour of the gods Poseidon and Zeus.

This, and the bull rhyton from the tholos tomb at Porti Mesaras (Xanthoudides, 1924, 62, pl. VII:5052), bear the earliest depictions in Minoan art of the wild bull *Bos primigenius Creticus* and the custom of bull-leaping.

Scenes of bull-leaping have been found outside Crete throughout the entire Mycenaean world, at Mycenae, Tiryns, Orchomenos, Vapheio, Athens and elsewhere.

Eleni Banou

Bibliography:

A Reichel. 'Die Stierspiele in der Kretisch-Mykenischen Kultur', *AM XXXIV*, 1909, 85–99.

St Xanthoudides. *The vaulted tombs of Mesara*, London, 1924, pls II, VII.

C Davaras, *A guide to Cretan antiquities*, Park Ridge, 1976, 32, fig. 20.

SEAL IMPRESSION

Cat no. 3

Provenance: palace at Pylos

Late Helladic IIIB (13th century BC)

Clay

1.7 (h) x 2.1 (diam) cm

National Archaeological Museum, Athens, 8476

On the main side of this seal impression of irregular shape with a hole pierced through it along the long axis is a relief scene of a boxing match. A man is turned to the right, his legs wide astride and his fists aimed at his opponent's jaw. The latter, at the edge of the field, faces the attack with his fists clenched in front of his waist. About one-quarter of the seal impression is missing.

The scene is dominated by the first figure, with its large size, strong movement and the frontal rendering of the chest. The second figure, whose movements are more restrained, seems to have been portrayed in a defensive attitude. The Minoan origins of the subject are attested by the Ayia Triada rhyton and the 16th-century BC wall-painting of the boxing boys from Santorini (Thera).

Maria Vlassopoulou-Karydi

Bibliography:

A Sakellariou. *CMS I*, 1964, 344, no. 306.

A Sakellariou. *Μυκηναϊκή Σφραγιδογλυφία*, Athens, 1966, 65.

37

MODEL OF A CHARIOT

Cat no. 4

Provenance: Mycenae, chamber tombs

Late Helladic IIIB (13th century BC)

Clay

10 (h) x 12 (l) x 5 (w) cm

National Archaeological Museum, Athens, 2262.

The presence of the chariot in the Mycenaean artistic repertoire, in the Linear B tablets, and especially on grave stelae, sarcophagi and vases found in graves, reflects its importance in the Mycenaean world, and probably also the practice of holding chariot races in honour of distinguished men who had died, attested by the Homeric poems.

This stylised model consists of a chariot with two riders, drawn by two horses. The horses' legs are connected in pairs and have conical ends. Their necks are yoked together. From the yoke hang the reins, which end at the riders' chests. The heads of the latter project above the semicircular front of the chariot. The model is slightly damaged and has been mended and restored.

Maria Vlassopoulou-Karydi

Bibliography:

Ch. Tsountas. *Ανασκαφαί τάφων εν Μυκήναις, ΑΕ*, 1888, p 170.

J H Crouwel. *Chariots and other means of land transport in Bronze Age Greece*, 1981, Amsterdam, pp 145, 147.

A Sakellariou-Xenaki. *Οι Θαλαμωτοί Τάφοι των Μυκηνών*, 1985, p 162, no. Π 2262, pl. 63.

BOEOTIAN KRATER

Cat no. 5

Provenance: Thebes

690–670 BC

Clay

34 (h) cm

National Archaeological Museum, Athens, 12896

Boxing was one of the oldest sports, and is first mentioned as a sporting contest by Homer in his description in *The Iliad* (XXIII, 681 ff.) of the funeral games held in honour of Patroklos.

Both sides of the krater are decorated with a depiction of a boxing match. Each of the opponents wears a boxing glove, and one is portrayed as fatter than the other. The scene is flanked by warriors watching the contest, wearing their swords at the waist and holding their horses by the reins. The spaces between the figures are occupied by geometric patterns.

Rosa Proskynitopoulou

Bibliography:

G Nicole. *Catalogue des vases pcints du Musée National d'Athènes*, Paris, 1911, p 131, no. 785.

F Canciani, Böotische. Vasen aus dem 8 und 7 Jahrhundert, *Jdl* 80, 1965, p 32, no 2.

J N Coldstream. *Greek Geometric pottery*, London, 1968, p 205, no. 12, pl. 44:g, j.

CVA Tübingen 1, p 20 ('Winkel-Gruppe').

O Tzachou-Alexandri (ed.). *Mind and body: athletic contests in ancient Greece*, catalogue of the exhibition, Athens, 1989, p 128, no. 24 (R Proskynitopoulou).

ATTIC AMPHORA

Cat no. 6

Provenance: unknown (probably Attica)

Attributed to the workshop of Athens, 897

720–700 BC

Clay

32 (h) cm

National Archaeological Museum, Athens, 18135

Empedokles Collection

On the neck of this amphora is a depiction of two horses confronting each other from either side of a tripod cauldron, to the handles of which they are tied. Beneath the animals' bellies are water birds. The spaces in the scene, and the entire amphora, are covered with geometric patterns.

From the time of Homer tripods were offered as parting gifts to official visitors, and also, like horses, as valuable prizes for victors in the games (*Iliad* XXIII, 259–60). Their significance as prizes and as objects sacred to Apollo meant tripod cauldrons were very frequently dedicated in sanctuaries.

The amphora would have had a lid.

Rosa Proskynitopoulou

Bibliography:

S Benton. 'The evolution of the tripod-lebes', *BSA*, 35, 1934–1935, p 103, no. 2, pl. 25:2.

J N Coldstream. *Greek Geometric pottery*, London, 1968, p 78, no. 17.

O Tzachou-Alexandri (ed.). *Mind and body: athletic contests in ancient Greece*, catalogue of the exhibition, Athens, 1989, pp 306–7, no. 195 (R Proskynitopoulou).

ATTIC GEOMETRIC PYXIS

Cat no. 7
Provenance: unknown
750–735 BC
Clay
26 (h) cm
National Archaeological Museum, Athens, 17604

These kinds of vessels were usually placed in graves as offerings, or contained the ashes of people who had been cremated. The handle on the lid takes the form of four plastic horses with their eyes and reins also painted. From a very early period the horse was a symbol of the aristocracy, though it was also associated with the cult of the dead. In this particular case, they possibly symbolised the four-horse chariot in which their owner had taken part in a chariot race. It is highly likely that he was the victor in the race, in which case the horses as symbolised on this pyxis would have been the prize awarded for his triumph.

Rosa Proskynitopoulou

Bibliography:

O Tzachou-Alexandri (ed.). *Mind and body: athletic contests in ancient Greece*, catalogue of the exhibition, Athens, 1989, p 126, no. 22 (R Proskynitopoulou).

RELIGION AND MYTHOLOGY

Religion permeated every facet of life in the city-state, and athletics were no exception. Sporting events in ancient Greece were held in honour of the gods and participants believed that to win they needed the gods' support in addition to ability. The Olympic Games essentially honoured Olympian Zeus and the first day of the games was devoted to religious observance and festivities, including the official opening with the slaughter of a pig in the temple of Zeus. Over the carcass, athletes and judges pronounced the Olympic oath of fair play. Amongst the sporting events was the sacrifice of 100 oxen on the third day, the fifth and final day was devoted to prize-giving, processions, and an evening banquet for the victors.

Displaying mortal frailty, depictions of gods and heroes in ceramics and sculpture provided a rich background of physical competition. The origins of the Olympic Games have been attributed to a chariot race between the mythical hero Pelops and King Oinomaos at Olympia, which is depicted on the east pediment of the temple of Zeus. One legend about the origins of the Pythian Games at Delphi was the battle to the death between Apollo and the serpent Python. These and other stories, such as the mythical hero Herakles' competitive endeavors, became part of popular culture, ingrained into the ancient psyche. The temple of Zeus at Olympia features, in sculptural relief, Herakles' 12 labours of atonement for his misdeeds which frequently called upon his prowess in wrestling and boxing and, as seen here, were popular subjects in sculpture and vase painting.

Paul Donnelly

STATUETTE OF A MALE FIGURE, PROBABLY ZEUS

Cat no. 8
Provenance: sanctuary of Zeus at Olympia, found in 1880
About 520 BC
Bronze
29 (h) cm
National Archaeological Museum, Athens, X 6163

This figure exudes an air of sobriety, tranquility and majesty. The statuette was the creation of an artistic workshop in the north-east Peloponnese, possibly at Corinth. The god wears a long himation thrown over his left shoulder, beneath which the body is delineated. His long hair is secured by a thin diadem with an astragal pattern. He walks forward with his left leg advanced and in each hand he would have been gripping some object that is now lost — possibly a spear in the right and a sceptre or sword in the left.

Rosa Proskynitopoulou

Bibliography:

Olympia IV, nos 40 and 40a, pl. VII.

E Walter-Karydi. *Die Äginetische Bildhauerschule: Werke und schriftliche Quellen, Alt-Ägina II*, 2, Mainz, 1987, pp 94ff., figs 139–140 (for the workshop).

O Tzachou-Alexandri (ed.). *Mind and body: athletic contests in ancient Greece*, catalogue of the exhibition, Athens, 1989, p 238, no. 129 (P Calligas).

I Vokotopoulou. *Ελληνική Τέχνη, Αργυρά και Χάλκινα Έργα Τέχνης* Ekdotike Athenon, Athens, 1997, p 229, no. 48.

VOTIVE RELIEF

Cat no. 9

Votive relief

Provenance: Athens

About 410 BC

Marble

70 (h) x 69 (w) cm

National Archaeological Museum, Athens, 1389

The relief was probably dedicated in the Pythion, near the Olympieion temple in Athens, and depicts the three Delian gods. In the centre, Apollo is seated majestically on the sacred tripod. At the right, his mother Leto, dressed in a peplos, looks at the god and rests her right hand on his shoulder. The figure on the left, whose head is missing, is Apollo's sister Artemis, who is drawing back her himation with her left hand and has her right resting on her bow. The missing top left corner has been restored with plaster.

Nikolaos Kaltsas

Bibliography:

I N Svoronos. *Das Athener Nationalmuseum*, Athens, 1908, pp 334–5, pl. 54.

Chr Karusos. *AM 54*, 1929, 4, no. 6.

LIMC II, 265, no. 657 (Apollon).

O Tzachou-Alexandri (ed.). *Mind and body: athletic contests in ancient Greece*, catalogue of the exhibition, Athens, 1989, p 228, no. 118 (V Machaira).

G Güntner. *Göttervereine und Götterversammlungen auf attische Weihreliefs*, Würzburg, 1994, 155 E3, pl. 32, 2.

L E Baumer. *Vorbilder und Vorlagen*, Acta Bernesia XII, Bern, 1997, 126, R17, pl. 28.

E Vikela. *AM 112*, 1997, 206, pl. 27, 4.

INSCRIBED DISCUS

Cat no. 10

Provenance: Olympia, south of the north-west gate to the Altis, found in 1879.

3rd century AD

Bronze

34 (diam.) x 1.4 (h) cm

Ancient Olympia Museum, M 891, K 656, Br 7567

The discus was dedicated to Zeus by Publius Asklepiades, victor in the pentathlon. Both sides are decorated with concentric circles and bear inscriptions. The inscription on one side records the name of the dedicator, Publius Asklepiades of Corinth, winner of the pentathlon at the 255th Olympiad (in AD 241): ΕΥΧΑΡΙΣΤΗΡΙΟΝ ΔΙΕΙ ΟΛΥΜΠΙΩΙ ΠΟΠΛ[ΙΟΣ] ΑΣΚΛΗΠΙΑΔΗΣ ΚΟΡΙΝΘΙΟΣ ΠΕΝΤΑΘΛΟΣ ΑϹΝΕ (In thanks to Olympian Zeus from Publius Asklepiades of Corinth, Pentathlete).

The inscription on the other side contains the ratification by the *alytarches*, Flavius Scribonianus, to whom the votive was delivered, who boasts that he is related to senators and consuls: ΔΙΙ ΟΛΥΜΠΙΩΙ ΑΛΥΤΑΡΧΟΥ ΦΛ[ΑΒΙΟΥ] ΣΚΡΕΙΒΩΝΙΑΝΟΥ ΣΥΝΓΕΝΟΥΣ ΣΥΝΚΛΗΤΙΚΩΝ ΚΑΙ ΥΠΑΤΙΚΩΝ ΟΛΥΜΠΙΑΔΟΣ ΥΝΣΤ (To Olympian Zeus, from the *alytarches* Fl[avius] Scribonianus, relative of senators and consuls).

Each side of the discus numbers the Olympics differently. The 255th is counted from the conventional date of 776 BC, whereas the other side names that Olympiad as the 456th — a date that gave the games an even more distant and mystical beginning in mythology.

Xenia Arapoyianni

Bibliography:

A Fürtwängler. *Olympia IV: die Bronzen und die Übrigen Kleineren Funde von Olympia*, 1966, 179.

Jüthner. *Die Athletischen Leibesübungen der Griechen*, Vienna, 1968, 239, fig. 60.

H V Herrmann. *Olympia Heiligtum und Wettkampfstätte*, Munich, 1972, 188, fig. 130.

'TYPE B' ATTIC RED-FIGURE KYLIX

Cat no. 11

Provenance: unknown

About 500 BC

Clay

8.8 (h) x 22.5 (rim diam) cm

National Archaeological Museum, Athens, 1666

Donated by Charilaos Trikoupis

The outside of the kylix depicts two mythical heroes, who served as models for young men, embodying the ideals of physical prowess and excellence of character and giving expression to the spirit of competition. On one side Herakles wrestles with the menacing giant Antaios. In the spaces the inscription ΑΘΕΝΟΔΟΤΟΣ ΚΑΛΟΣ (Athenodotos the fair) can be seen. On the other side Theseus, holding an axe in his right hand, has defeated Procrustes, who is on his knees, wounded in the side. The inscription ΚΑΛΟΣ (fair) is painted in the spaces.

Rosa Proskynitopoulou

Bibliography:

ARV², pp 1567–8, no. 13.

T Sekl. *Untersuchungen zum Verhältnis von Gefässform und Malerei attischer Schalen*, Berlin, 1985, p 54, no. 273, pl. 49:1.

O Tzachou-Alexandri (ed.). *Mind and body: athletic contests in ancient Greece*, catalogue of the exhibition, Athens, 1989, pp 134–5, no. 29 (R Proskynitopoulou).

ATTIC BLACK-FIGURE AMPHORA

Cat no. 12

By the Painter of Villa Giulia M482

Provenance: Exarchos, Locris

520–500 BC

Clay

23.5 (h) x 10.6 (rim diam.) cm

National Archaeological Museum, Athens, 446

Side A features a depiction of Herakles wrestling with the sea daemon Triton, son of Poseidon. The contest is flanked by two onlookers wearing himatia and holding staffs. The figure at the left has been identified with Nereus, the old man of the sea. The hero has immobilised his opponent between his legs and is applying the 'knot' hold, gripping him tightly around the chest with both arms. Triton is facing left and raises his right hand towards the hero's head in an effort to break free.

This scene of Herakles wrestling with Triton or Nereus was one of the most popular in Attic vase-painting, especially black-figure painting, and was almost invariably rendered in an identical manner. Although the reason for the wrestling contest between the hero and Nereus is well known — to discover the secret route to the distant land of Hesperides (Pherekydes) — there is no literary source referring to a similar contest with Triton.

Elisabeth Stassinopoulou-Kakarouga

G Ahlberg-Cornell. *Herakles and the sea-monster in Attic black-figure vase-painting*, Stockholm 1984, Group XI 9.

O Tzachou-Alexandri (ed.). *Mind and body: athletic contests in ancient Greece*, catalogue of the exhibition, Athens, 1989, p 132, no. 28 (R Proskynitopoulou).

THE GYMNASIUM

The gymnasium was an educational facility that was used as a sports ground and as a school. As a public institution it was open to all citizens (free men) and was usually located in a sacred grove beside a stream, as is the case in Olympia. Significantly, the gymnasium of the ancient Greeks was expected to exercise both body and mind. Such principles are upheld in the mythical tradition of the zenith of Greek heroes, Achilles, whose knowledge and aptitude for music and sport allowed the Homeric ideal — 'always to be best and excel over others' — to prevail. It was at gymnasiums in Athens that the philosopher Plato and Aristotle established schools (the Academy and Lyceum) in the 4th century BC.

In terms of physical organisation, it seems that the track events were taught in the gymnasium, whereas jumping and the combat sports (wrestling, boxing and *pankration*) were taught in the palaestra. This was an enclosed area frequently associated with, or part of, the gymnasium which was usually a privately run training ground. Around a sandy courtyard for training were rooms for undressing, washing, boxing punch-bags, ball games, dusting before exercise and storing cleansing oil. *Gymnos* means to go naked and training, like competition, was conducted naked. A state of undress, as commented upon by Thucydides, was considered by the ancient Greeks to be characteristic of their civilisation. The representation of nakedness seen in the selection of objects in this section is further complicated by the notion that nakedness conferred heroic status; an association that grieving relatives sought to perpetuate in their choice of grave markers, but possibly did not provide a real likeness of the deceased.

Paul Donnelly

'PROTO A' TYPE ATTIC BLACK-FIGURE KYLIX

Cat no. 13

From the workshop of the Lydos Painter

Provenance: Exarchos, Locris

About 550–540 BC

Clay

13.7 (h) x 24 (rim diam) cm

National Archaeological Museum, Athens, 445

Purchased in 1882

Both sides of the kylix depict young athletes training for the pentathlon in the gymnasium or palaestra. At the left is a discus-thrower with the discus side-on in his right hand, while a long-jumper runs to the right, holding *halteres* (jumping weights) in both hands. Other figures with their right fists clenched and their left hands raised may be runners. The other side of the kylix depicts a boxer winding boxing thongs around his hands in preparation for a contest. Between the athletes on both sides are figures of youths, either naked or wearing himatia.

Rosa Proskynitopoulou

Bibliography:

ABV, p 113, no. 83.

CVA Athènes 3, pp 57–8, pls 48–9.

O Tzachou-Alexandri (ed.). *Mind and body: athletic contests in ancient Greece*, catalogue of the exhibition, Athens, 1989, p 154, no. 42 (R Proskynitopoulou).

ATTIC RED-FIGURE BELL KRATER

Cat no. 14

Provenance: unknown

First quarter of the 4th century BC

Clay

22.5 (h) x 23.3 (rim diam) cm

National Archaeological Museum, Athens, 17920

Both sides depict scenes from the palaestra. On the left of side A are two naked athletes holding their equipment — an *aryballos* or oil container, and a strigil, used for cleaning the body after exercise. They run towards their bearded trainer, who awaits them standing upright, wearing a himation and holding the characteristic staff. The basic task of the trainer was to prepare and train the young men so they were in a good physical condition and would perform at their best in their specialised event or events. On side B two youths wearing himatia converse next to a colonnette, which is a symbol of the palaestra.

Elisabeth Stassinopoulou-Kakarouga

Bibliography:

O Tzachou-Alexandri (ed.). *Mind and body: athletic contests in ancient Greece*, catalogue of the exhibition, Athens, 1989, p 170, no. 56 (R Proskynitopoulou).

'TYPE C' ATTIC RED-FIGURE KYLIX

Cat no. 15

Provenance: unknown (Athens?)

Middle of the 5th century BC

9 (h) 22.4 (rim diam) cm

National Archaeological Museum, Athens, 17302

This kylix depicts scenes from the palaestra. At the centre of the scene on side A a young, naked athlete offers an *aryballos* (oil container) to a fellow athlete who is undressing in preparation for training. Next to the athlete undressing is the javelin. Their tutor leans on his staff and looks on.

On side B, a tutor and a young athlete holding a strigil watch a javelin-thrower, who is putting his fingers in the *angyle* (the leather loop-strap that will help him throw his javelin straight and steadily). A pair of sandals, *aryballoi* (oil containers) and strigils hang in the background.

Elisabeth Stassinopoulou-Kakarouga

Bibliography:

CVA Athènes 2, III Id, pls 13,2–4 and 15,4.

O Tzachou-Alexandri (ed.). *Mind and body: athletic contests in ancient Greece*, catalogue of the exhibition, Athens, 1989, p 164, no 50.

HEAD OF A YOUTH

Cat no. 16

Provenance: Athenian Acropolis, probably found in 1866

About 480–470 BC

Bronze

11 (h) cm

National Archaeological Museum, Athens, X 6590

This head, which comes from a statuette of a youth, is a superb work of art, full of power, grace, nobility and sobriety. It probably comes from a major workshop in the north-east Peloponnese. The hair is wound around a thin band low on the forehead and ears, and is gathered in a bun at the nape of the neck. Pure copper was used for the band in the hair, the eyebrows and the lips. The eyes were made of a different material and inlaid. The statuette was dedicated in the sanctuary of Athena on the Acropolis, probably by a young athlete.

Rosa Proskynitopoulou

Bibliography:

A de Ridder. *Catalogue des bronzes trouvés sur l'Acropole d'Athènes*, Paris, 1896, p 288, no. 767, figs 274–5, pl. VI.

E Walter-Karydi. *Die Äginetische Bildhauerschule: Werke und schriftliche Quellen, Alt-Ägina II*, 2, Mainz, 1987, p 88, no.5 (Korinthisch), p 92, figs 127–8 (for the workshop).

O Tzachou-Alexandri (ed.). *Mind and body: athletic contests in ancient Greece*, catalogue of the exhibition, Athens, 1989, p 176, no. 67 (P Calligas).

D Buitron-Oliver (ed.). *The Greek miracle: Classical sculpture from the dawn of democracy, the fifth century BC*, catalogue of the exhibition, Washington, 1992, pp 90–1, no. 6.

PART OF A GRAVE STELE

Cat no. 17

Provenance: Piraeus, from the area of Halai, found in 1836

First half of the 4th century BC

Marble

44 (h) x 33.5 (w) cm

National Archaeological Museum, Athens, no. 873.

The scene on this fragment from the middle of a stele with a relief representation of a *loutrophoros* (a funerary vase carved with a relief depiction) is set in the palaestra, as indicated by the pillar standing on a pedestal. A young, naked athlete practises a game that is not depicted or documented in any other ancient representation or literary source. He is trying to balance a ball on his right knee, with the leg bent at a right angles. He stands on his left leg, his weight on his toes, with his right arm behind his back gripping his left wrist, probably to keep his balance. In front of him, the young slave-attendant holding his master's strigil and *aryballos* (oil container) looks on in admiration.

Nikolaos Kaltsas

Bibliography:

A Conze. *Die attischen Grabreliefs II*, Berlin, 1900, no. 1046, pl. 203.

R Stupperich. *Staatbegräbnis und Privatgrabmal im klassischen Athen*, Münster, 1977, 110, 118, 156, no. 46.

G Kokula. 'Marmorlutrophoren', *AM 10, Beih.*, 1984, 152, L1, pl. 3,1.

O Tzachou-Alexandri (ed.). *Mind and body: athletic contests in ancient Greece*, catalogue of the exhibition, Athens, 1989, p 199, no. 90 (V Machaira).

Ch Clairmont. *Classical Attic tombstones*, Kilchberg, 1993, no. 1890.

STATUETTE OF HERAKLES

Cat no. 18

Provenance: Athens

Third quarter of the 4th century BC

Marble

54 (h) cm

National Archaeological Museum, Athens, 253

As the founder of athletic games, Herakles was venerated particularly in training grounds, such as gymnasia, stadia and palaestras, where statues of him and hermaic stelae bearing his head were erected. The demigod, son of Zeus and Alkmene, is depicted standing naked, and wearing the lion-skin, which covers his head, is fastened on his chest and gathered on his left arm. He would have been holding his club in his left hand. The forearms are missing from roughly below the elbows and the legs from the knee down.

Nikolaos Kaltsas

Bibliography:

B Graef. *RM 4*, 1889, 199–200, no. 23.

LIMC IV, 749, no. 377, pl. 470 (Herakles).

O Tzachou-Alexandri (ed.). *Mind and body: athletic contests in ancient Greece*, catalogue of the exhibition, Athens, 1989, p 150, no. 39 (V Machaira).

GRAVE STELE

Cat no. 19

Provenance: Lavrion, Attiki, found in 1925

Middle of the 4th century BC

Marble

1.28 (h) m

National Archaeological Museum, Athens, 3586

The dead athlete depicted in this stele, which has the form of a small temple with antae and a pediment, was Theophrastos, son of Theophrastos from the deme of Halai, as we learn from the inscription carved on the epistyle. He is shown relaxing after his training in the palaestra, naked and leaning against a pillar. In his left hand he holds the strigil with which he will scrape the dust from his body if he hasn't already done so. In front of him stands his young slave, who has his master's himation draped over his shoulder and is holding an *aryballos* (oil container) for him.

Nikolaos Kaltsas

Bibliography:

S Karouzou. *National Archaeological Museum, collection of sculpture*, catalogue, Athens, 1968, p 72.

O Tzachou-Alexandri (ed.). *Mind and body: athletic contests in ancient Greece*, catalogue of the exhibition, Athens, 1989, pp 339–40, no. 229 (V Machaira).

Ch Clairmont. *Classical Attic tombstones*, Kilchberg, 1993, no. 1879.

GRAVE STELE

Cat no. 20

Provenance: Tanagra, Boeotia, found in 1904

Early 4th century BC

1.37 (h) m

Marble

National Archaeological Museum, Athens, 2578

This stele would have stood above the grave of an athlete. It has the form of a small temple with antae and a crowning member on which two sphinxes are depicted with a palmette between them. The dead man, who was called Stephanos, as we are informed by the inscription carved on the epistyle, was depicted standing naked, with a himation thrown over his left shoulder, accompanied by his dog. In his left hand he holds a strigil and an *aryballos*, two essential pieces of an athlete's equipment.

Nikolaos Kaltsas

Bibliography:

V Schild-Xenidou. *Boiotisch Grab- und Weihreliefs, archäischer und klassischer Zeit*, Thesis, Munich, 1972, 52, no. 58.

U Vedder. *Untersuchungen zur plastischen Ausstattung attischen Grabanlagen des 4 Jhs v. Chr.*, Frankfurt, 1985, 261 (A15).

O Tzachou-Alexandri (ed.). *Mind and body: athletic contests in ancient Greece*, catalogue of the exhibition, Athens, 1989, p 179, no. 70 (V Machaira).

G Despinis. *Egnatia 3*, 1991–1992, 12.

Ch Clairmont. *Classical Attic tombstones*, Kilchberg, 1993, no. 1214.

STRIGILS

Cat no. 21 *(bottom left)*
Provenance: Eretria, found in 1886
5th–4th century BC
Bronze
17 cm
National Archaeological Museum, Athens, X 8302

Strigils had a variety of uses in connection with both male and female hygiene, and were essential equipment for athletes, who used them after training to cleanse their bodies of sand, dust, sweat and the oil with which they had been covered. This strigil consists of a distinctly curved scraper or blade and a handle, which is fastened to its spine by means of an attachment in the form of an ivy leaf.

Rosa Proskynitopoulou

Bibliography:

A de Ridder. *Catalogue des bronzes de la Société Archéologique d'Athénes*, Paris, 1894, p 110, no. 564.

O Tzachou-Alexandri (ed.). *Mind and body: athletic contests in ancient Greece*, catalogue of the exhibition, Athens, 1989, p 173, no. 62 (P Calligas).

Cat no. 22 *(top left)*
Provenance: probably Keratsini, Piraeus
5th–4th century BC
Bronze
17 cm
National Archaeological Museum, Athens, X 8632
Purchased in 1877

This strigil is fastened to its handle by means of an attachment in the form of an ivy leaf (similar to cat. no. 21). The wider part of the handle is stamped with the name ΕΡΜΩΝ (Hermon), possibly that of the owner.

Rosa Proskynitopoulou

Bibliography:
A de Ridder. *Catalogue des bronzes de la Société Archéologique, d'Athénes*, Paris, 1894, p 107, no. 532.

O Tzachou-Alexandri (ed.). *Mind and body: athletic contests in ancient Greece*, catalogue of the exhibition, Athens, 1989, p 174, no. 63 (P Calligas).

Cat no. 23 *(right)*
Provenance: Plataea, found in 1868
Late 2nd – early 1st century BC
Bronze
25 cm
National Archaeological Museum, Athens, X 8283

This strigil is more strongly curved than those of cat. nos 21 and 22, and has a folded, closed, rectangular handle. The handle is threaded on a flattened bronze ring, split at one point, on which the strigil was suspended and carried.

Rosa Proskynitopoulou

Bibliography:

A de Ridder. *Catalogue des bronzes de la Société Archéologique, d'Athénes*, Paris, 1894, p 111, no. 572.

O Tzachou-Alexandri (ed.). *Mind and body: athletic contests in ancient Greece*, catalogue of the exhibition, Athens, 1989, p 174, no. 65 (P Calligas).

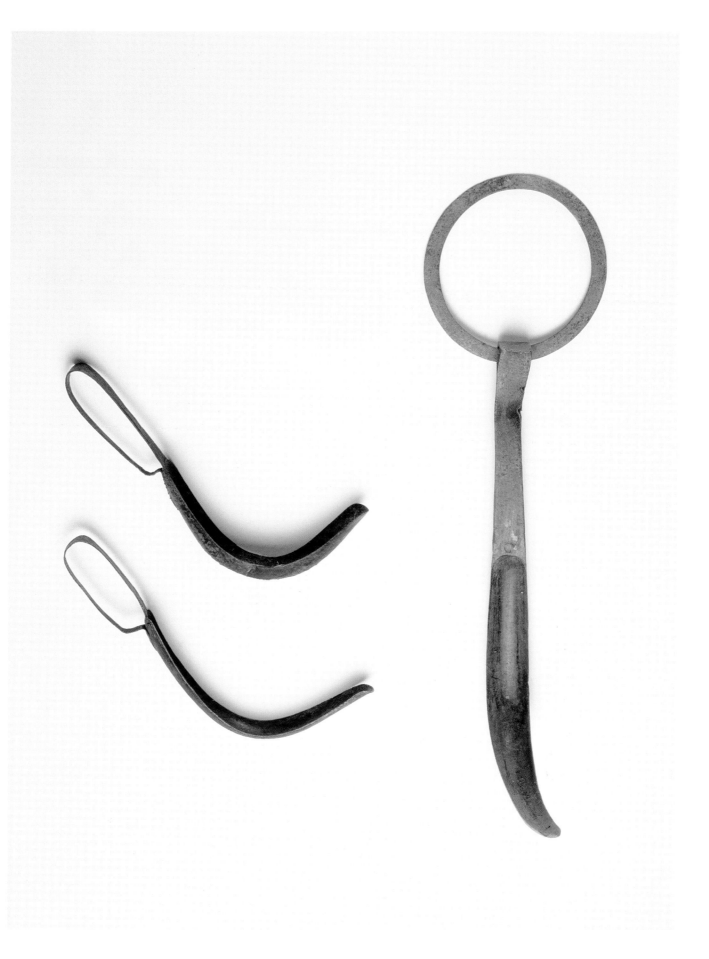

RELIEF BASE OF A FUNERARY STATUE OF A KOUROS

Cat no. 24

Provenance: Athens, found built into the
Themistoclean Walls in 1922

About 510 BC

Marble

29 (h) x 79 (w) cm

National Archaeological Museum, Athens, 3476

The base originally supported a statue of a *kouros*, which is evident from the socket in the top, in which the plinth was inserted. It has relief scenes on three of the four sides, all of them set in the training ground of the gymnasium and palaestra. The centre of the scene on the front is occupied by two athletes engaged in a wrestling contest. One has gripped his opponent's left arm in what was called 'the ram's hold', and the other is trying to push him off. On the left, another athlete is making a jump, while the one on the right is holding a javelin.

The left side of the base depicts six athletes in different events and exercises. The figure on the extreme left is preparing to throw a ball, watched by one of his fellow athletes. In the centre are two runners: the one with his palms open is taking part in the *stadion* (sprint race), while the other, with clenched fists, is running in the *dolichos* (distance race). The two athletes on the right are gesticulating as they look on.

The scene on the right side of the base is set in the changing rooms of the gymnasium or paleastra and shows four youths dressed in himatia and holding staffs. The two in the centre are sitting on stools called *diphroi ochladias*, inciting a dog and a cat to fight.

Nikolaos Kaltsas

Bibliography:

A Philadelpheus. *AD 6*, 1920–1921, 1–11, figs 1–4.

A Philedelpheus. *BCH 46*, 1922, 1–17, figs 1–4, pls 1–3.

LaRue Van Hook. *AJA 30*, 1926, 283–7.

W Deyhl. *AM 84*, 1969, 16, 25, pl. 25.

G Schmidt. *AM 84*, 1969, 71–5, pl. 27.

W Fuchs and F Floren. *Die Griechische Plastik I*, Munich, 1987, 293–4, pl. 26, 5.

O Tzachou-Alexandri (ed.). *Mind and body: athletic contests in ancient Greece*, catalogue of the exhibition, Athens, 1989, pp 278–80, p 167 (V Machaira).

D Viviers. *Recherches sur les ateliers des sculpteurs et la Cité d'Athénes à l'époque archaïque*, [Brussels], 1992, 190–2, 200–1, 212–13, fig. 51.

FOOTRACES

Footraces were the earliest competitions of the Olympics, dating to when the games lasted a single day, rather than the eventual five. Footraces were undertaken over varying distances, with the original being the *stadion*, a fast sprint over one length of the track (around 200 m). The first 13 Olympics after 776 BC consisted only of this race and it remained one of the most prestigious throughout the history of the ancient Olympic Games, with each Olympiad named after the winner of this event. In 724 BC the *diaulos* was introduced, a race twice the length of the *stadion*. The longest race was the *dolichos*, which varied between 1400 and 3800 m, and was thought to have derived from the heralds, professional runners who carried news, including the announcement of the Sacred Truce throughout the country.

Importantly, the footrace is one of the few recorded official sports in which women participated. In Olympia a festival called the Heraia was held between the Olympiads in honour of Hera, Zeus's wife, whose temple at Olympia predated that of Zeus. The Heraian race was five-sixths of a *stade* and was divided into different classes according to age.

A visually spectacular variation on the footrace, which emphasises the games' military connection, was the *hoplitodromos* (racing soldiers in armour). This race was two lengths of the track and competitors were partially clad in armour, wearing helmet and greaves, and carrying a shield.

Paul Donnelly

STATUETTE OF A RUNNER

Cat no. 25
Argive workshop
Provenance: archaeological site of ancient Olympia, found in 1936
480–470 BC
Bronze
10.2 (h) cm
Ancient Olympia Museum, B26

This statuette, along with four others — a discus-thrower (cat. no. 32), a long-jumper, a javelin-thrower and a wrestler, seems to have formed a votive offering made by an Olympic victor in the pentathlon, probably Dandes of Argos, a well-known winner in the *dolichos* (long-distance race) in 476 BC and the *stadion* (sprint) in 472 BC.

The athlete is depicted naked, standing on a low square base. His body leans forward in a starting position. His left foot is slightly raised in front of him and he holds out his arms just below the chest, with the right elbow slightly bent. The youthful face is framed by short hair and the large eyes gaze steadily ahead, giving the athlete an expression of decisiveness and inner concentration. A votive inscription to Zeus, ΤΟ ΔΙFΟΣ ΙΜΙ (I belong to Zeus), is incised on the outside of his right thigh.

Xenia Arapoyianni

Bibliography:

Olympia Ber. I, Armin von Gerkan. *Die Vorbereitende Grabung in Olympia*, 1936–1937, 20, 47–8, figs 12–13, 41–2.

G M A Richter. *Archaic Greek art*, New York, 1949, 191, fig. 293.

G Lippold. *Die griechische Plastik, Handbuch der Archäologie*, Munich, 1950, 100, note 17.

Jüthner. *Die athletischen Leibesübungen der Griechen*, Vienna, 1968, 69, note 135, pl. 12a.

A Mallwitz. *Olympia und seine Bauten*, Munich, 1972, 57, fig. 61.

H Herrmann. *Olympia, Heiligtum und Wettkampfstätte*, Munich, 1972, figs 3a–b.

K Palaeologos. 'Running', *The Olympic Games in ancient Greece*, Athens, 1986, p 156, fig. 66.

STATUETTE OF AN ATHLETE

Cat no. 26

Provenance: Athenian Acropolis, found in 1883

About 470–460 BC

Bronze

16.5 (h) cm

National Archaeological Museum, Athens, X 6614

The statuette, which was probably made by an Attic workshop, was evidently dedicated as a tithe by Philaios in the sanctuary of Athena on the Acropolis, perhaps after a victory in games held in the goddess's honour.

The figure has been variously interpreted as a runner, a long-jumper or a discus-thrower. Perhaps it is a long-jumper who has just released the *halteres* (jumping weights) that he was holding and is attempting his jump. On both sides of his body there is a dotted votive inscription: ΗΙΕΡΟΣ: ΤΕΣ ΑΘΕΝΑΙΑΣ / ΦΙΛΑΙΟ: ΔΕΚΑΤΕΝ (Sacred to Athena: Philaios (or Philaithos) [dedicated me as] a tithe).

Rosa Proskynitopoulou

Bibliography:

A de Ridder. *Catalogue des bronzes trouvés sur l'Acropole d'Athènes*, Paris, 1896, pp. 275-7, figs 257–8.

H G Niemeyer. *Attische Bronzestatuetten der spätarchaischen und frühklassischen Zeit, Antike Plastik III*, Berlin, 1964, pp 26–7, pls 21 and 35b.

O Tzachou-Alexandri (ed.). *Mind and body: athletic contests in ancient Greece*, catalogue of the exhibition, Athens, 1989, pp 261–2, no. 154 (P Calligas).

I Vokotopoulou. *Ελληνική Τέχνη, Αργυρά και Χάλκινα Έργα Τέχνης*, Ekdotike Athenon, Athens, 1997, p 254, no. 132.

ATTIC BLACK-FIGURE KYLIX

Cat no. 27

By the Painter of Athens 533 (name vase*)

Provenance: Corinth

570–560 BC

Clay

10 (h) x 22.3 (rim diam) cm

National Archaeological Museum, Athens, 533

In the tondo inside the kylix, a young athlete runs to the right with his head turned back, possibly to see how far behind the other runners are. His wide stride and the vigorous movement of his arms are typical of sprint events such as the *stadion* (single length of stadium) or *diaulos* (double length of stadium). On the outside of the kylix are cockerels between sirens, men wearing himatia and lions.

* The painter has been named after this vase. It is against this object that other unsigned vessels are attributed.

Elisabeth Stassinopoulou-Kakarouga

Bibliography:

CVA Athènes 3, pls 4-5.

O Tzachou-Alexandri (ed.). *Mind and body: athletic contests in ancient Greece*, catalogue of the exhibition, Athens, 1989, p 244, no 136 (R Proskynitopoulou).

STATUETTE OF A GIRL RUNNING (*dromas*)

Cat no. 28

Provenance: sanctuary of Zeus at Dodone

Middle of the 6th century BC

Bronze

12 (h) cm

National Archaeological Museum, Athens, Kar. 24

Karapanos Collection

This statuette is the product of a Lakonian workshop and would have adorned the rim or shoulders of a large vase, to which it was attached by two rivets in the feet.

The young athlete wears a short chiton, belted at the waist, with short sleeves. She raises the hem slightly with her left hand, probably to make it easier for her to run. The characteristic features of the figure are the expressive face, the pronounced musculature and the youthful power of her sturdy, athletic body. She was probably taking part in a race for women.

Rosa Proskynitopoulou

Bibliography:

C Carapanos. *Dodone et ses ruines*, Paris, 1878, p 31, no. 4, pl. XI:1.

J Sweeney, T Curry and Y Tzedakis (eds.). *The human figure in early Greek art*, catalogue of the exhibition, Athens, 1988, p 133, no. 46 (Rosa Proskynitopoulou).

Le corps et l'esprit, catalogue de l'exposition, Lausanne, 1990, p 137, no. 91 (Rosa Proskynitopoulou).

I. Vokotopoulou. *Ελληνική Τέχνη, Αργυρά και Χάλκινα Έργα Τέχνης*, Ekdotike Athenon, Athens, 1997, pp 235–6, no. 70.

ATTIC BLACK-FIGURE PSEUDO-PANATHENAIC AMPHORA

Cat no. 29
Provenance: Kamiros on Rhodes,
Makry Langoni, tomb 182
About 500 BC
Clay
34 (h) x 13 (rim diam) x 11 (base diam) cm
Rhodes Archaeological Museum, 13281

This amphora is a smaller version of the large amphorae given to winners in the Panatheniac Games, which were held every four years in Athens as part of the annual festival honouring the goddess Athena. These 'pseudo' types were possibly made as souvenirs, or to serve some other market needs, funerary grave goods included. The rarity of real prize amphorae would have made them rare and expensive.

Appropriately, the goddess Athena is on the main side (not pictured), standing fully armed and stepping forward in a pose that gives her the name, Athena *Promachos* (in front of the battle line). On Athena's shield are two painted dolphins and the goddess is flanked by two Doric columns on which cockerels sit. The inscription on the ground of the amphora ΚΑΛΗ (fair) probably refers to the goddess. The other side (pictured) features three runners in poses with clenched fists and low-held arms that suggest they are participating in the *dolichos* (long-distance) race.

The neck of the amphora is decorated with alternating palmettes above a raised ring where the neck joins the shoulder.

Pavlos Triantafyllidis

Bibliography:

Clara Rhodos IV, 133–4, figs. 128, 129, 130.

O Tzachou-Alexandri (ed.). *Mind and body: athletic contests in ancient Greece*, catalogue of the exhibition, Athens, 1989, pp 248–9, no. 141 (P Valavanis), with bibliography.

PENTATHLON

As the name suggests, the event was composed of five sports. Three of them, discus, javelin and long jump, were only held as part of the pentathlon, whereas the footrace and wrestling were events in their own right. The footrace, javelin, discus and long jump were considered 'light' events, while wrestling was a 'heavy' event. According to Aristotle, 'the pentathletes are the best, because they are naturally endowed with both strength and speed'.

The footrace in the pentathlon was one length of the *stadion* (about 200 m). Most unfamiliar to modern eyes is the long jump, in which athletes used weights known as *halteres* to give additional momentum. The details are not recorded, but it is thought the weights were only an advantage in a standing rather than a running jump. The discus varied in size and weight, eventually averaging around 4–5 kg in weight and 17–31 cm in diameter, with smaller ones for the boys' event. Javelin throwing's obvious military connections, were more apparent in games at festivals other than the Olympics, such as the Panathenaic Games in Athens. In Athens, athletes mounted on a moving horse threw a javelin at a target, mimicking a cavalry tactic of the 4th century BC. In both kinds of event a thong attached to the middle of the shaft gave extra velocity to the throw.

It is probable that victory in the pentathlon relied on winning at least three events rather than all five.

Paul Donnelly

PART OF A GRAVE STELE

Cat no. 30
Provenance: Athens, Kerameikos cemetery, near the Dipylon gate, found in 1873
About 550 BC
Marble
35 (h) x 44 (w) cm
National Archaeological Museum, Athens, 38

This fragment from the top of a very tall grave stele is one of the finest and most important works of art from the Archaic period. All that is preserved of the relief representation is the face of a young discus-thrower holding the discus in his left hand. The head is masterfully projected against the circle of the discus and the facial details are rendered by superb working of the marble surface. It is thought to be the work of a major sculptor of unknown name who is conventionally known as the Rampin Master.

Nikolaos Kaltsas

Bibliography:
A Conze. *Die Attischen Grabreliefs I*, 1893, no. 5, pl. 4.
Ch Karousos. *BSA 39*, 1938–1939, 99–101.
E Harrison. *Hesperia 15*, 1956, 31, pl. 7.
G M A Richter. *The Archaic gravestones of Attica*, 1961, 19, no. 21, figs 72–6.
B Schmalz. *Griechische Grabreliefs*, 1983, 168, pl. 2,1.
D Viviersk. *Recherches sur les ateliers des sculpteurs et la cité d'Athènes à l'époque Archaïque*, 1992, 210–11.

STATUETTE OF A YOUTH

Cat no. 31

Provenance: Athenian Acropolis, found in 1888

About 500 BC

Bronze

27 (h) cm

National Archaeological Museum, Athens, X 6445

The statuette, which was dedicated in the sanctuary of Athena on the Acropolis, was the gifted work of an Athenian who was evidently influenced by works created in the north-east Peloponnese. It probably depicts a youth taking part in the long jump, moving forward to start his jump. In both hands he held *halteres* (jumping weights) in front of his body. His expression exudes the nobility, power, and self-confidence of the young athlete. The short, delicately engraved hair is bobbed on the forehead and at the nape of the neck, leaving the ears exposed.

Rosa Proskynitopoulou

Bibliography:

A de Ridder. *Catalogue des bronzes trouvés sur l'Acropole d'Athènes*, Paris, 1896, pp 268–9, no. 740.

H G Niemeyer. *Attische Bronzestatuetten der spätarchaischen und frühklassischen Zeit, Antike Plastik III*, Berlin, 1964, pp 24–5, pls 17–19, 33b–c.

J Sweeney, T Curry and Y Tzedakis (eds). *The human figure in early Greek art*, catalogue of the exhibition, Athens, 1988, p 134, no. 47 (Rosa Proskynitopoulou).

Le corps et l'esprit, catalogue de l'exposition, Lausanne, 1990, p 183, no. 148 (Rosa Proskynitopoulou).

I Vokotopoulou. *Ελληνική Τέχνη, Αργυρά και Χάλκινα Έργα Τέχνης*, Ekdotike Athenon, Athens, 1997, p 239, no. 83.

STATUETTE OF A DISCUS-THROWER

Cat no. 32

Provenance: archaeological site of ancient Olympia

480–470 BC

Bronze

9.7 (h) cm

Ancient Olympia Museum, B6767 + 7500

This statuette is apparently one of the four that, together with the statuette of the runner (cat. no. 25), formed a votive offering in the sanctuary made by an Olympic victor in the pentathlon, possibly Dandes. It was probably made in an Argive workshop in the Peloponnese.

The athlete stands on a low square base with his body leaning backwards as he prepares to throw the discus with his right hand and raises his left arm for balance. The left leg is drawn behind, supporting the weight of the body. A votive inscription, ΤΟ ΔΙFΟΣ ΙΜΙ (I belong to Zeus), is incised on the left thigh.

The statuette was found in 1965 in two pieces: the upper body and thighs, and the base with the lower legs. The surface is corroded, mainly at the back of the head, left arm, left shoulder and left leg. The arms are missing from about the middle of the forearms.

Xenia Arapoyianni

A Mallwitz, H V Herrmann. *Die Funde aus Olympia*, Athens, 1980, p 157, no. 107, 2.

DISCUS

Cat no. 33

Provenance: Olympia, west of the Bouleuterion, found in 1880.

About 6th–5th century BC

Bronze

16.5 (diam) x 0.1 (d) cm; 1.877 kg

Ancient Olympia Museum, M892, K658

Discus-throwing was one of the events in the pentathlon and one of the favourite sports of the Greeks. It was introduced into the Olympic Games in 655 BC, and the first victor was the Spartan pentathlete Lampes. The event demanded rhythm, precision and strength. Discuses were originally made of stone, and later of iron, lead or bronze. They were round or biconcave, with a broad rim and a diameter ranging from 17 to 31 cm. Their weight differed from city to city, though in the games the competitors all threw the same discus in the interest of fairness. The surfaces of discuses were often engraved with artistic scenes, verses, odes and even texts of treaties.

The ancient technique of discus-throwing was similar to that practised today, and the results were recorded on the ground by wooden markers and then measured with poles. The young athlete Phlegyas is said to have thrown the discus from one bank of the river Alpheios to the other. The earliest evidence for discus-throwing comes from Homer's *Iliad*, where it is mentioned in the context of the games organised by Achilles in honour of the young Patroklos.

This well-preserved discus is quite light compared with those usually used in this event, which weighed about 4–5 kg. It was presumably used by athletes in training.

Xenia Arapoyanni

Ekbotiki Athenon (ed.). *The Olympic Games in ancient Greece*, 1982, pp 188–90.

Elisabeth Spathari, *The Olympic spirit*, Athens, 1992, pp 111–12.

PAIR OF HALTERES (JUMPING WEIGHTS)

Cat no. 34

Provenance: Corinth

Late 6th – early 5th century BC

Stone

23–24 (l) cm; 2.018 kg

National Archaeological Museum, Athens, 1926

Halteres made of either stone or metal were used in the long jump to give greater momentum. Evidently both their shape and weight were important factors. Long-jumpers held *halteres* in their hands as they executed their jump and threw them backwards when they were in mid-air to achieve greater forward impetus. These *halteres* belong to the Archaic type, with one convex side and the other sides virtually flat. The elliptical holes were for the athlete's fingers. Athletes holding *halteres* can be seen on the Attic red-figure lekythos (cat. no. 35) and the red-figure kylix (cat. no. 38).

Nikolaos Kaltsas

Bibliography:

K Mylonas. *AE 1884*, 104.

S Karousou. *National Archaeological Museum, collection of sculpture, catalogue*, Athens, 1968, p 30.

E N Gardiner. *Athletics of the ancient world*, Oxford, 1967, p 146.

O Tzachou-Alexandri (ed.). *Mind and body: athletic contests in ancient Greece*, catalogue of the exhibition, Athens, 1989, pp 175–6, no. 66 (V Machaira).

ATTIC RED-FIGURE LEKYTHOS

Cat no. 35

By the Bowdoin Painter

Provenance: unknown (possibly Athens)

475–470 BC

Clay

18.3 (h) cm

National Archaeological Museum, Athens, 17281

A young, naked, beardless long-jumper is depicted above a band of 'meander' pattern on this lekythos. He holds the *halteres* (jumping weights) in his hands and his body is bent forward with his left leg in front of his right as he prepares to jump. The expressive face reveals his concentration and confidence in the outcome of his effort. On the ground before him is a discus bearing an owl and the inscription ΔΑΜΟΣΙΟΣ (?) (public). His cleansing equipment, a sponge, a strigil and an *aryballos* (oil container) are depicted at the top of the scene.

Rosa Proskynitopoulou

Bibliography:

CVA Athènes 2, p 10 (III Ic-d), pl. 12:6,7.

ARV², p 684, no. 145.

O Tzachou-Alexandri (ed.). *Mind and body: athletic contests in ancient Greece*, catalogue of the exhibition, Athens, 1989, pp 161–2, no. 48 (R Proskynitopoulou).

ATTIC RED-FIGURE LEKYTHOS

Cat no. 36

Manner of the Providence Painter

Provenance: probably Athens

About 470–460 BC

Clay

15.7 (h) cm

National Archaeological Museum, Athens, 17280

On this lekythos a naked athlete is depicted facing right, preparing to throw the javelin he holds in his right hand at the side of his head. The athlete, who has short hair and a thin, youthful beard, takes a wide stride in order to gain momentum while balancing himself by extending his left arm.

Rosa Proskynitopoulou

Bibliography:

ARV², p 645, no. 2.

E Sermbeti-Papoutsaki. *O Ζωγράφος της Providence,* Athens, 1983, pp 231, 235.

O Tzachou-Alexandri (ed.). *Mind and body: athletic contests in ancient Greece*, catalogue of the exhibition, Athens, 1989, p 266, no. 159 (R Proskynitopoulou).

ATTIC BLACK-FIGURE KYLIX (SIANA CUP)

Cat no. 37

By the Sandal Painter

Provenance: Ritsona, tomb 49

540–530 BC

Clay

13.7 (h) x 33 (rim diam) x 24.7 (greatest diam without handles) x 33.6 (greatest diam with handles) x 9 (base diam) cm

Thebes Archaeological Museum, R49.261 (6113)

On side A is a javelin-throwing scene with six spectators. A naked athlete faces right preparing to throw the javelin. He is flanked by two naked youths who look on, raising their left arms.

The scene on side B depicts a boxing match with five spectators. The contestants confront each other in the normal stance for boxers, standing firmly on the ground with their legs apart and their arms extended or drawn back behind their heads ready to deliver the next punch. Wound around their arms are leather thongs, called *strophia* or *meilichai* in ancient Greek.

The tondo inside the kylix is encircled by a band of tongue pattern and features a depiction of a naked, bearded male figure running to the left.

Anastasia Gadolou

Bibliography:

J D Beazley. *ABV*, 1956, 70, 2.

K Demakopoulou and D Konsola. *Οδηγός αρχαιολογικού Μουσείου Θήβας*, Athens, 1981, fig. 3.

O Tzachou-Alexandri (ed.). *Mind and body: athletic contests in ancient Greece*, catalogue of the exhibition, Athens, 1989, p 266, no. 158 (E Kakarouga - Stassinopoulou).

P N Ure. 'Black-figure kylikes from Rhitsona in Boeotia', *AE*, 1915, 114–27, 116–117, fig. 1.

For a Siana cup with a similar boxing scene by the same painter, see *CVA Baltimore 1*, 41, pl. 20.1.

RED-FIGURE KYLIX

Cat no. 38

Attributed to the Antiphon Painter

Provenance: Athens

Around 490 — 480 BC

Clay

10 cm (h) x 30 cm (width over handles)

Powerhouse Museum, Sydney, 99/117/1

The painted scenes on this kylix relate to the pentathlon and victory. On side A *(right)*, a naked youth is holding a discus, and behind him another youth appears to be exercising using *halteres* (jumping weights). To the right of the two athletes a trainer keeps a watchful eye. Side B *(detail left)* depicts two naked athletes, one holding *halteres*. They flank a trainer who appears to be instructing or settling a dispute between the two.

In the medallion of the cup is a youth reclining on a couch. He is wearing a victor's wreath and is attending a symposium (drinking party). He is playing *kottabos*, a boisterous game of wishful thinking in which the dregs of a wine cup were flicked across the room into a vessel (or at a desired person) while a name was said aloud: in this case 'Laches' is written as if spoken from the youth's mouth. Other words on the cup refer to Laches' beauty, such as 'ho pais kalos' (the boy is beautiful). In ancient Greece, athletes were considered the ultimate objects of beauty and desire, and Laches is the most popular *kalos* name used on the 100 or so cups attributed to the Antiphon Painter.

Paul Donnelly

Bibliography:

Francois Lissarrgue. 'Publicity and performance: *kalos* inscriptions in Attic vase-painting' in Simon Goldhill and Robin Osborne (eds), *Performance, culture and Athenian democracy*, Cambridge University Press, Cambridge, 1999, p 369

J Boardman. *Athenian red-figure vases: the Archaic period*, Thames and Hudson, London, 1975, p 135

J D Beazley. *Attic red-figure vase painters*, vol I, 2nd edn, Clarendon Press, Oxford, 1963, pp 335 – 41.

COMBAT

The dramatic combat sports of wrestling, boxing and *pankration* were popular with spectators. Many athletes were adept in two or more of these sports, but rarely won them in the same Olympiad. In sculpture or on pottery these athletes are depicted with disfigurements caused by their sport — broken noses, cauliflower ears and scars — human attributes on otherwise idealised representations.

Wrestling was both part of the pentathlon and an independent event. There were two styles of wrestling: upright and ground. Three throws won the upright version and conceding defeat decided the victor of the ground variety. The many different grips and manoeuvres were taught in textbooks and in training, which was conducted in an area named after one of the mythological inventors of the sport, Palaestra, daughter of Hermes. It was a wrestler, Milon of Kroton, whose six wins made him the most renowned of any athlete ever to compete at Olympia.

The frescoes of boxers on Santorini (Thera) indicate the sport dates from at least the 16th century BC, but there are many differences between ancient and modern practice. In ancient Greece there was no ring and therefore very little close fighting; there were no rounds so the pace was slow; and there was no weight matching so inevitably the larger competitor had a greater chance of winning. Hand protection (*himantes*) became increasingly offensive with time. After the fourth century BC the protective soft leather thong wrapped around the hand and arm was replaced by hard leather with sharp edges capable of cutting. The Romans introduced the *caestus*, a particularly dangerous glove weighted with iron and lead.

The *pankration* was reputed to have been invented by the hero Theseus, who combined wrestling and boxing to defeat the ferocious Minotaur, the bull-headed man of the labyrinth at Knossos in Crete. The *pankration* was akin to all-out fighting: holding the opponent while hitting him was allowed, but an umpire attended to prevent biting and gouging, the only forbidden manoeuvres in an event in which contestants occasionally were killed.

Paul Donnelly

HEAD OF A MALE STATUE

Cat no. 39
Provenance: south of the gymnasium, Olympia
340 BC
Pentelic marble
27 (h) cm
Ancient Olympia Museum, Λ99

This head presumably comes from the statue of a wrestler or *pankratiast*, as is clear from the cauliflower ears. The style of the figure seems to have been influenced by the schools of Skopas and Lysippos, when Classical idealism had already given way to realism. Emotive expressions and poses seen in art of this time reflected an awareness of existential problems and philosophical debate.

The athlete is beardless and his head is turned slightly to his left. The short, fine tresses of hair were tied with a band. The athlete's eyes are sunk deep in the sockets and his mouth is half-open from his final effort to win. The face and nose are considerably chipped. A large triangular piece missing from the top of the head was probably inlaid.

Xenia Arapoyianni

Bibliography:

G Lippold. *Die Griechische Plastik: Handbuch der Archäologie*, Munich, 1950, p 264, note 10.

K Schauenburg. *Athletenbilder des vierten Jahrhunderts v. Chr.*, Berlin, 1963, p 77, note 11.

G Treu. *Die Bildwerke von Olympia in Stein und Thon*, 1966, p 208, figs 17–19.

T B Dohrn. *Die Marmor-Standbilder des Daochos-Weihgeschenks in Delphi (Antike Plastik)*, Berlin, 1968, p 44, note 50, figs 17–19.

F Johnson. *Lysippos*, Durham NC, 1927, p 236, pl. 52 A–B.

STATUETTE OF A BOXER

Cat no. 40

Provenance: unknown

1st century BC

Bronze

14.6 (h) cm

National Archaeological Museum, Athens, Kar 546

Karapanos Collection

The boxer is depicted as a mature, bearded athlete with a muscular body. On his hands he wears the simple thongs (*himantes*) of the type called *meilichai* or *strophia*, which were made of long strips of soft oxhide. These protected the fighter's wrist and fingers when he was landing punches. His expression suggests that he was weary and had probably been defeated. The meaning of the gesture of the raised right hand is unknown, though it may have been a signal given during the contest.

Rosa Proskynitopoulou

Bibliography:

V Stais. *Marbres et Bronzes*, Paris, 1907, p 312.

O Tzachou-Alexandri (ed.). *Mind and body: athletic contests in ancient Greece*, catalogue of the exhibition, Athens, 1989, p 288, no. 176 (P Calligas).

ARM FROM A STATUE OF A BOXER

Cat no. 41

Provenance: found in the Antikythira shipwreck in 1900

Late 2nd – 1st century BC

Bronze

75 (preserved length) cm

National Archaeological Museum, Athens, X 15111

The soft working of the muscles on this larger-than-life-size left arm suggests that it probably belonged to a statue of a boy boxer. Fairly hard, thick thongs are wound around the first phalanx of the fingers, the thumb and some distance up the wrist. At the knuckles they are reinforced with rings of tougher leather to make the punches landed on the opponent more effective.

Rosa Proskynitopoulou

Bibliography:

R C Bol. *Die Skulpturen des Schiffsfundes von Antikythera*, Berlin, 1972, pp 34–5, pl. 18:1–2.

O Tzachou-Alexandri (ed.). *Mind and body: athletic contests in ancient Greece*, catalogue of the exhibition, Athens, 1989, p 287, no. 175 (P Calligas).

COIN, SILVER STATER

Cat no. 42

Provenance: city of Aspendos, Pamphylia (modern Belkis, province of Antalya, Turkey)

Around 385 – 370 BC

Silver

22 (diam) mm; 10.83 g; die axis ↓

Powerhouse Museum, Sydney, 99/80/1

The front of this coin depicts two wrestlers confronting each other *(right)*. The wrestler on the left holds the left arm of the other with both hands, and his opponent grips his right wrist. The letters 'ME' between the figures are probably the initials of the magistrate who was the issuing authority. The reverse *(below)* depicts a male slinger about to discharge a missile (usually a lead pellet) from his catapult. To the right is a three-legged *triskeles* symbol, and to the left a Greek inscription that translates as 'Eslevedius', an early name for Aspendos.

The design of this coin preserves aspects of life that were significant to the inhabitants of Aspendos, a maritime city of great wealth and importance at the time. It was a place noted for its wrestlers and this is one of the few Olympic contests to be featured on any coin. Aspendos was also famed for its hoplite infantry (soldiers), including its slingers who may be distinguished on these coins because of the similarity in sound of the Greek name for sling (*sphendone*) with Aspendos.

Pat Boland OAM, ED

Bibliography:

D R Sear. *Greek coins and their values, Vol II, Asia and North Africa*, Seaby, London, 1979 (reprinted 1996), p 491, no. 5390

G F Hill. *Catalogue of the Greek coins in the British Museum: Lycia, Pamphylia and Pisidia*, Arnaldo Forni, Bologna, 1897 (1964 facsimile), p 96, no. 20

S Von Aulock. *Sylloge Nummorum Graecorum Deutschland: Pamphylien 4477 — 4893*, Verlag Gebr. Mann, Berlin, 1965, compare no. 4555.

PART OF A GRAVE STELE OF A BOXER

Cat no. 43

Provenance: found in the Themistoclean Walls
between Kerameikos and the Hill of Nymphs.

About 540 BC

Marble

23 (h) x 33 (w) x 10 (d) cm

Kerameikos Museum, P 1054

This grave stele of a boxer, of which the head and part of the
wrist are preserved, is thought to have been of great
importance to the development of the art of portraiture in the
early Classical period. The deformed, hooked nose, the
swollen ear and the strong wrist wound with boxing thongs
define the figure and give it the personal features of an
athlete. They go far beyond the idealised characteristics
ordinarily attested at this period in Archaic art.

The large almond-shaped eye is framed by a strongly
delineated arching eyebrow. The mass of short hair, on
which tool marks are visible, ends in a wavy outline on the
forehead and stretches down to the nape of the neck at the
back. Both hair and beard are treated as single flat masses.

Vasiliki Orphanou

Bibliography:

N Yalouris. *Ελληνική Τέχνη. Αρχαία Γλυπτά.*, 1994,
p 236, no. 54.

Threpsiadis. *Ανασκαφικαί έρευναι εν Αθήναις*, PAE 1953, p 69ff.,
no. 7.

Chr Karouzou. *Αριστόδικος*, 1961, p 43ff.

W Fuchs and J Floren. *Die Griechische Plastik*, vol. I, Munich, 1987,
p 285, fig. 23,8.

G M A Richter. *The Archaic gravestones of Attica*, London, 1961,
p 23ff., no. 31, fig. 92.

B Schmaltz. *Griechische Grabreliefs*, Darmstadt, 1983, 169, pl. 2, 2.

ATTIC RED-FIGURE AMPHORISKOS OF PANATHENAIC SHAPE

Cat no. 44

By the Pythokles Painter

Provenance: Aegina

Early 5th century BC

Clay

19.5 (h) x 12.6 (belly diam) cm

National Archaeological Museum, Athens, 1689

Side A of this amphoriskos depicts Athena *Promachos* (frontline of the battle), standing with her back to the viewer and her head turned to the left. She wears armour, holds a spear in her right hand and carries a shield on her left arm upon which is the emblem with Pegasos.

The boxing match depicted on side B *(right)* is in its concluding stages. The boxer on the right is going down to the punch landed by his opponent's left hand. As the loser falls he gives the sign for conceding the contest by raising the index finger of his right hand. The boxers' hands are wound with soft thongs.

In contrast to the heavy bodies and deformed features of mature boxers, these youths have athletic, compact bodies. They would have systematically trained from childhood to acquire harmonious physiques.

Elisabeth Stassinopoulou-Kakarouga

Bibliography:

O Tzachou-Alexandri (ed.). *Mind and body: athletic contests in ancient Greece*, catalogue of the exhibition, Athens, 1989, p 285, no. 173 (R Proskynitopoulou).

EQUESTRIAN EVENTS

The equestrian events were prestigious and spectacular. Only the wealthy could participate since horses and chariots were very expensive to purchase and maintain, but the renown of winning was immense. Philip II, father of Alexander the Great, was so proud of his two Olympic wins that he minted coins depicting and celebrating his victories, yet he didn't even go to Olympia. It was the owner, not the jockey or charioteer, who was named for posterity as winner of the events in the hippodrome (horseracing stadium), which explains why women, children and towns are sometimes named as victors on the lists carved in marble. The hippodrome at Olympia is known only through the description given by the chronicler Pausanius (in about AD 150), since it was washed away by the river Alpheios. No other hippodromes in Greece survive for comparison or as a model.

The early pictorial and modelled ceramic references to chariots and horses reflect their military and social significance to the aristocracy wealthy enough to own them. By the time equestrian events were formally organised, there were many varieties of events. At the Olympic Games, different combinations of two- and four-horse chariots were introduced at different times, as well as races in which chariots were drawn by foals or mules. Races of horses, foals and mules, ridden by naked jockeys, were also staged. There were further variations at games other than Olympia, including dramatic events requiring dismounting — another legacy of battle. The race for apobatai (particularly popular in Athens) required a semi-armoured warrior (apobates) to dismount and remount a chariot moving at speed. The distinctive spectacle and technique have been successfully captured in sculptural reliefs. The kalpe, which was held for a brief time in Olympia, required a rider to dismount during the race and run with the horse over the finishing line.

Paul Donnelly

FRAGMENT OF A VOTIVE RELIEF

Cat no. 45

Provenance: sanctuary of Amphiaraos at Oropos, Attica, found in 1887

About 400 BC

Marble

59 (h) x 39 (w) cm

National Archaeological Museum, Athens, 1391

This fragment depicts a scene from a chariot race. The chariot, charioteer and an *apobates*, who is depicted naked, wearing only a helmet, are preserved. The *apobates* holds a shield in his left hand and grips the rail of the chariot with his right, his body leans backwards, tensed and ready to jump from the speeding chariot. The skill of the *apobates* was to remain upright during this dangerous manoeuvre and then dash for a distance beside the chariot (while avoiding those around him) to eventually remount. Inevitably the race for *apobatai* was a spectacular event, and its danger seemed particularly appropriate at religious festivals.

This fragment was found at Oropos in the sanctuary of the mythical Amphiaraos, where it had probably been offered by a victor in the races dedicated to this hero.

Nikolaos Kaltsas

Bibliography:

N Papadakis. *AE 1910*, 252–66, pl. 11.

I N Svoronos. *Das Athener Nationalmuseum*, Athens, 1908, pl. 56.

V Ch Petrakos. *Ὁ Ωρωπός και το ιερόν του Αμφιαράου*, Athens, 1968, 121, no. 17, pl. 39.

E Mitropoulou. *Corpus I: Attic votive reliefs of the 6th and 5th centuries BC*, Athens, 1977, no. 132, fig. 192.

O Tzachou-Alexandri (ed.). *Mind and body: athletic contests in ancient Greece*, catalogue of the exhibition, Athens, 1989, pp 297–9, no. 186 (V Machaira).

INSCRIBED BASE

Cat no. 46
Provenance: Athens, post-Herulian Wall, south of the
Stoa or Attalos and below the Eleusinion, 1933
Early 4th century BC
Pentelic marble
39 (h) x 91 (w) x 44 (d) cm
Ancient Agora Museum, S 399

A prize for a chariot race in the Panathenaic Games was
fixed into the rectangular socket in the top of this marble
base, while two smaller rectangular sockets to the right and
left were for other objects. The name of the prizewinner, Krates,
son of Heortios, from Piraeus is inscribed on the top band.

The contest is depicted in the relief on the front of the base.
A four-horse chariot is shown moving towards the left and
the charioteer is holding the reins in both hands. The hoplite
apobates is making his jump and has his right foot on the
moving chariot, while the left one still hangs down. The
horses, which are staggered in different postures with their
heads differentiated, are good examples of Classical art,
though the charioteer and *apobates* are rendered only
summarily. The style of the scene and the letter forms date
the base to the early 4th century BC.

Alkestis Spetsieri-Choremi

Bibliography:

T L Leslie Shear. *AJA XXXVI*, 1933, 542, fig. 3.
Hesperia IV, 1935, 379–81, fig. 8.

H A Thompson. *The Athenian Agora XIV*, 1972, 121.
The Athenian Agora guide, 1990, 207–8.

PSEUDO-PANATHENAIC BLACK-FIGURE AMPHORA

Cat no. 47

Late 5th century BC

Provenance: Stoa of Attalos, in a well in shop 3.

Reddish clay

27.7 (h) x 11 (rim diam.) x 18 (belly diam.) x 9 (base diam.) cm

Ancient Agora Museum, P 24661

The amphora features a scroll of palmettes and lotus-flowers on the neck, tongue pattern on the shoulder and ray ornament on the lower part of the body. Side A depicts Athena striding to the left. She is wearing chiton, aegis and helmet. She holds out her shield with its device of two dolphins and brandishes her spear. She is flanked by two thin Doric columns, each surmounted by an owl. On side B a chariot is drawn by four horses galloping to the right. The bearded charioteer holds the reins in both hands and the whip in his right hand. The anatomical and other details have been incised and white paint has been used for details such as Athena's flesh, the device on the shield, the charioteer's chiton and the third horse.

Alkestis Spetsieri-Choremi

Bibliography:

H A Thompson. *Hesperia XXV*, 1956, p 62, pl. 21a.

Stella Miller. *Hesperia*, Supplement 20, p 96, pl. 14d.

M B Moore and M Z P Philippides. *The Athenian Agora*, p 23, 1966, no. 319, pl. 32.

AMPHOROID KRATER

Cat no. 48

Provenance: Mycenaean cemetery in the Nauplion area, chamber tomb B

Brownish-red clay

Late Helladic IIIB (13th century BC)

45.3 (h) x 34 (body diam) x 27 (rim diam) cm

Nauplion Archaeological Museum, 15180

The neck and base of the krater are painted solid black. There are horizontal bands on the belly and base, vertical bands on the spine of the strap-handles and chevrons and S-shaped lines on the flat rim. The scene extending over the shoulder on either side of the krater shows a chariot with two horses and two riders, moving to the left between stylised palm-trees. The riders are rendered in profile. The heads and necks of the figures are shaded, and the upper parts of their bodies and part of the chariot is rendered in outline. The lower part of the chariot consists of a wheel with four spokes.

Katerina Barakari

Bibliography:

AD 28, 1973, 90ff., pl. 90.

E Vermeule and V Karageorghis. *Mycenaean pictorial vase-painting*, Harvard University Press, Cambridge, Mass, 1982, p 88, 221, pl. IX,1.

Å Åkerström. *The pictorial pottery*, Berbati, II, Stockholm, 1987, pp 111ff., 117ff., figs 80,1, 82,2.

The Mycenaean world: five centuries of early Greek culture 1600–1100 BC, National Archaeological Museum, Athens, 15 December 1988 – 31 March 1989, p 243, no. 242.

RELIEF OF A HORSE AND RIDER

Cat no. 49
Provenance: sanctuary of Zeus at Dodone
About 550–540 BC
Bronze
82 (h) x 12 (l) cm
National Archaeological Museum, Athens, Kar 36
Karapanos Collection

Like athletes depicted on vases taking part in equestrian contests in the hippodrome, this young horseman rides naked. In full control of his galloping steed, he turns and directs a lively gaze at the spectator. With his whip in his right hand, he holds the reins firmly with his left.

The horse's mane and forelock are rendered as vertical tresses, and the tail is incised. The three small rivets in the animal's body indicate that the relief adorned the neck of an elaborate bronze krater dedicated in the sanctuary of Zeus Dodonaios, an epithet given to Zeus at his sanctuary at Dodone in the mountains of Epirus. The vase is attributed to a notable Corinthian metal workshop of the second half of the 6th century BC.

Mary Zaphiropoulou

Bibliography:

C Carapanos. *Dodone et ses ruines*, Paris, 1878, pl. 13,1,183.

I Vokotopoulou. *Χαλκαί Κορινθιουργείς Πρόχοι,* 1975, pl. 521, γ, 145.

S Karousou.*Τεχνουργοί κρατήρων, AM 94*, 1979, 77ff., pl. 13.

H Walter-Karydi. *Jb Berl. Museen*, 23, 1981, 20, fig. 12.

O Tzachou-Alexandri (ed.). *Mind and body: athletic contests in ancient Greece*, catalogue of the exhibition, Athens, 1989, pp 303–4, no. 192.

I Vokotopoulou. *Αργυρά και Χάλκινα Έργα Τέχνης*, 1997, 243, fig. 97 (Greek art).

STATUETTE OF A HORSE AND RIDER

Cat no. 50

Provenance: sanctuary of Zeus at Dodone

570–550 BC

Bronze

12.3 (total h) x 11.2 (l); 9.5 (h of rider);

10.8 (h of horse) cm

National Archaeological Museum, Athens, Kar 27 + X 16547

Karapanos Collection

The young rider looks straight ahead, holding the horse's reins, which, like the rider's right arm, have not survived. He wears a short, close-fitting chiton. The horse, which has a rich mane, is trotting gently.

The rider was found during Constantin Karapanos's excavations at Dodona in 1875 and the horse was found in 1935. A similar horse from the same sanctuary, now in the Louvre, seems to have been made for the rider from the Karapanos Collection. The group, dedicated to Zeus Dodonaios, probably depicted the Dioskouroi, the sons of Zeus who were brilliant horsemen, warriors and Olympic victors as mentioned by Pausanias (5, 8.4). The Dioskouroi come from a Corinthian metal workshop of the second quarter of the 6th century BC.

Mary Zaphiropoulou

Bibliography:

C Carapanos. *Dodone et ses ruines*, Paris, 1878, pl. 11,3,181 (rider).

S Karouzou. *Οι ιππείς της Δωδώνης , 'Θεωρία'* , Theoria: Festschrift, W. Schuchhardt, Baden-Baden, 1960, 231ff.

I Vokotopoulou. *Χαλκαί Κορινθιουργείς Πρόχοι*, 1975, pl. 521 α-β, 142, 145.

O Tzachou-Alexandri (ed.). *Mind and body: athletic contests in ancient Greece*, catalogue of the exhibition, Athens, 1989, pp 141–2, no. 32.

I Vokotopoulou. *Αργυρά και Χάλκινα Έργα Τέχνης*, 1997, 235, fig. 69 (Greek art).

STATUETTE OF A RIDER

Cat no. 51

Provenance: from the Heraion on Samos

Late 6th century BC

Bronze

19.3 (h) cm

Samos Archaeological Museum, B97-A1262

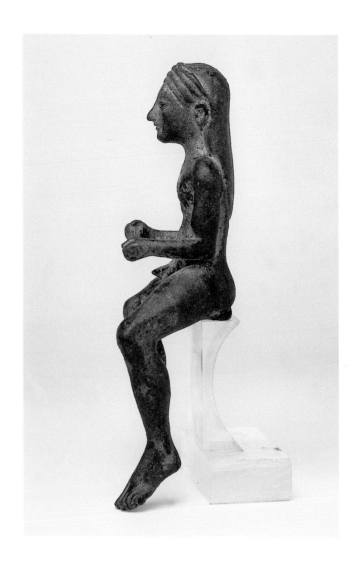

The subject of the horseman must have been popular in the Late Archaic period on Samos, as is clear from the discovery of a large number of votive bronze riders in the Samian Heraion, a sanctuary sacred to Hera. This statuette is a product of a Samian workshop from the last years of Polykrates or the time of his successors.

This statuette was probably part of a group. The facial features are rendered naturalistically and the eyes are inlaid. The rider's straight hair hangs to the middle of his back and ends in a semicircle. It is restrained on his forehead by a wreath adorned with three incised lines. The rider's arms are bent forward at the elbows and his hands are clenched, forming a hole for the reins.

Maria Viglaki

Bibliography:

E Buschor. *Altsamische Standbilder*, Berlin, 1960.

ATTIC BLACK-FIGURE KYLIX (SIANA CUP)

Cat no. 52

By the Taras Painter

Provenance: Corinth

About 560 BC

Clay

13.9 (h) x 26.6 (rim diam) cm

National Archaeological Museum, Athens, 530

Both sides of the kylix are decorated with equestrian events. Young horsemen, seated naked on the backs of their steeds, gallop to the left. The jockeys are riding bareback, without stirrups, as was usual in horseraces. On the tondo inside the cup Hermes runs to the left holding his caduceus.

Elisabeth Stassinopoulou-Kakarouga

Bibliography:

H A G Brijder. *Siana cups and Komast cups*, Mainz, 1983, p 250, no. 150.

Le corps et l'esprit, catalogue de l'exposition, Lausanne, 1990, p 159, no. 118 (N Kaltsas).

COIN, GOLD STATER

Cat no. 53

Provenance: probably Pella

323 – 317 BC, posthumous issue of Philip II (359 – 336 BC) minted during the rule of Philip III Arrhidaeus (323 – 317 BC)

Gold

18mm (diam); 8.59 g; die axis →

Powerhouse Museum, Sydney, 94/269/1

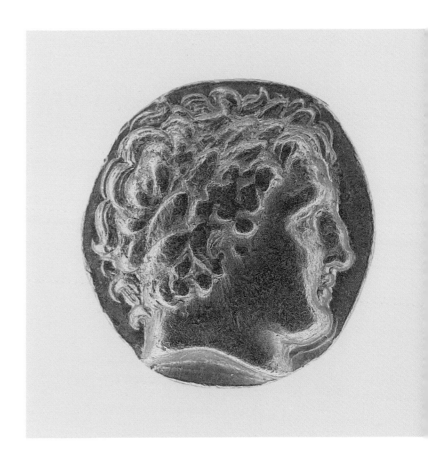

The reverse of this coin *(below)* features a chariot racing to the right, its charioteer coiled within the rim whipping the horses in a gallop to the finish. Just visible at the top is a victory wreath symbolising that this was no ordinary chariot, but an Olympic winner. Below the ground line (exergue) is the name Philip, and below the horse is a serpent and the monogram 'A' and 'Pi', identifying for the ancients where the coin was minted. On the front of the coin is the laureate (wreathed) head of the Greek god, Apollo.

This coin commemorates the victory of King Philip II in the *synoris* (two-horse) chariot race in 348 BC, and followed two earlier equestrian victories. This type of coin, issued long after Philip II's death in 336 BC, is the same type as that minted by him after his chariot victory. Perpetuating a prestigious Olympic victory was propaganda that suited Philip's successors as much as Philip himself. Plutarch (*Alexander* 4) notes Philip was personally responsible for the designs of his coins, and this coin is a reminder that the Olympics had played a part in establishing his reputation as the head of a dynasty, planning to conquer the world.

Paul Donnelly

Bibliography:

G Le Rider. *Le Monnayage d'argent et d'or de Phillipe II frappé en Macédoine de 559 à 294*, E Bourgey, Paris, 1977, compare nos. 600 – 2, p 193

I Carradice and M Price. *Coinage in the Greek world*, Seaby, London, 1988, pp 106 – 10

D R Sear. *Greek coins and their values: vol.II*, Asia and North Africa, Seaby, London, 1979 (reprinted 1996), p 617, compare no. 6663.

VOTIVE RELIEF

Cat no. 54

Provenance: Argos

Early 4th century BC

Marble

61 (h) x 37 (w) cm

National Archaeological Museum, Athens, 3153

A naked youth is depicted in low relief on a plain quadrilateral slab. Behind him, his horse is shown with its right foreleg raised. The youth is depicted in profile to the right with his body turned three-quarters and his head shown frontally; his right arm hangs down, his relaxed leg is drawn behind him, and he carries his spear over his shoulder. This pose is the earliest free rendering of the famous bronze statue of the Doryphoros (spear-bearer) by the 5th-century Argive sculptor Polykleitos about 440 BC.

This work is of great importance for the study of ancient Greek sculpture, and is known from the many copies made in the Roman period. It depicts Arcilles, the hero of the Homer poems, but is essentially the embodiment of the ideal youth. In it the static coexists with movement, the body is subjected to the spirit, and the proportions are in perfectly balanced harmony. It is for these reasons that Polykleitos called his work the Canon, and wrote an essay with this title in which he analysed the way it was made.

Nikolaos Kaltsas

Bibliography:

A Furtwängler. *AM 3*, 1878, 287ff., pl. 13.

A Milchhöfer. *AM 4*, 1879, 153–4, no. 502.

Th Lorenz. *Plyklet*, 1972, 54, pl. 21,4.

F Langenfass-Vuduroglou. *Mensch und Pferd auf griechischen Grab- und Votivsteinen*, Munich, 1974, 58, no. 113.

O Tzachou-Alexandri (ed.). *Mind and body: athletic contests in ancient Greece*, catalogue of the exhibition, Athens, 1989, p 338, no. 227 (V Machaira).

LIMC VI, 1025, no 5, pl. 673 (Heros Equitans).

BLACK-FIGURE NECK AMPHORA AND COVER

Cat no. 55

Attributed to the Group of Toronto 305 (Antimenes Painter Circle)

Provenance: Athens

About 520 BC

Clay

39.8 cm (h) 47cm (h with cover) x 26 (max diam) cm

Powerhouse Museum, Sydney, A4378

Gift of Sir Norman Rydge and Sir Robert Webster, 1952

Side A of this amphora *(left)* depicts the escorting of Ariadne (the bride of Dionysos) to their wedding ceremony. Two satyrs, some of the wild retinue of Dionysos, approach Ariadne, who is holding her veil in a traditional gesture of bridal modesty. Behind, and seemingly blossoming from Ariadne, are vines symbolising wine, Dionysos himself, and a fruitful afterlife.

On side B *(right)* are two youths in their late teens (*ephebes*) epitomising the appearance and activities of wealthy young Athenians. They are perfect products of the gymnasium, and both ride horses and carry spears in their right hands. Their nakedness in this non-competitive context is idealised in the manner of heroes, victorious athletes, or characters from myth, but there are no symbolic or written clues to confirm this.

Horses were a popular subject on black-figure vases, second only to humans in quantity of representation. For the three decades from 530 BC, black-figure continued alongside the newly developed red-figure technique. The influence of the new style is seen on this vase in the elongated height and slimmer proportions of the horses — a distinctive tendency of painters in the group associated with the Antimenes Painter, to which this amphora belongs.

Paul Donnelly

Bibliography:

J D Beazley. *Attic black-figure vase painters*, Clarendon Press, Oxford, p 283, no. 8 *bis*

Mary Moore. *Horses on black-figured Greek vases of the Archaic period, ca 620 – 480 BC*, University Microfilms, Ann Arbor MI, 1977, pp 402 –34

Andrew Stewart. *Art, desire and the body in ancient Greece*, Cambridge University Press, Cambridge, 1997, pp 80 –85.

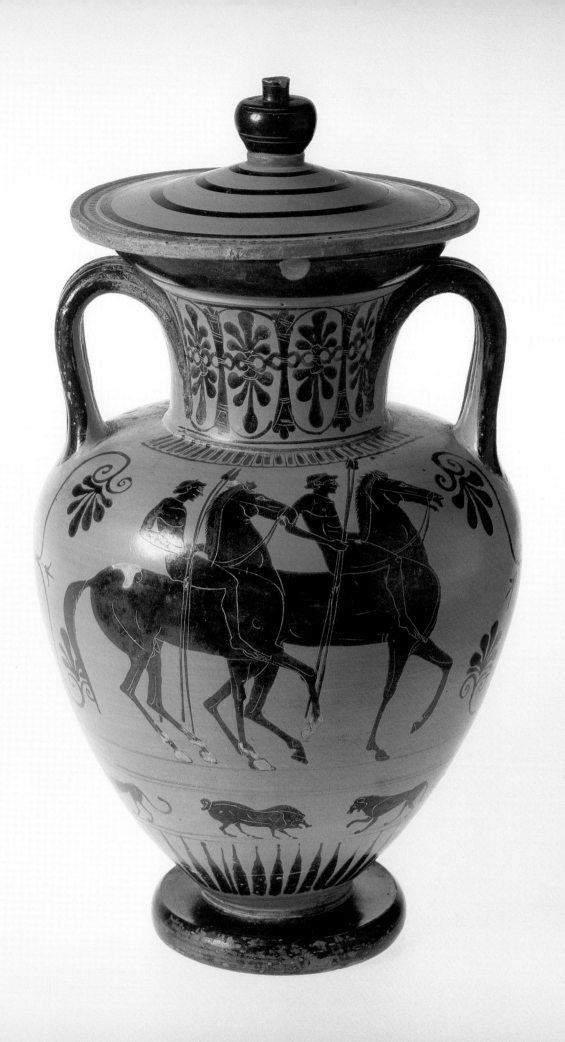

WINNING

'Here [in Olympia] he died, boxing in the stadium, having prayed to Zeus for either the wreath or death, Age 35. Farewell.'

Epitaph of Agathos Daimon, found near Olympia

To win was everything in the ancient Olympics, and the greatest prize was immortal fame. On the last day of the games, the victors, wearing red woollen ribbons, would receive their olive crowns in front of the temple of Zeus. Victors' statues were erected at Olympia, as well as in their home city, with three-times winners accorded the privilege of an accurate rather than an idealised likeness. Particularly successful athletes achieved hero status and were worshipped with sacrifices and gifts in the manner of the mythical heroes Theseus and Herakles.

Among the various prizes awarded at games, we are fortunate that the prizes given at the Panathenaic Games held in Athens were containers of oil. These amphorae depict the sports for which they were awarded and are an invaluable record of ancient sporting activities. Winning was also depicted by ceramic painters with Nike, a winged personification of victory, bestowing the crown upon the winner.

While training must have played a part, it was thought that victory was possible only through the favour of the gods. Gifts to the gods, in the form of (often engraved) miniature bronze statues of athletes, equipment (such as a discus) or marble sculptural reliefs were dedicated in thanks for victory. Gratitude was sincere, especially considering that, in addition to honour and status, an Olympian victor was assured of great wealth, as well as prestigious civic honours and privileges.

Paul Donnelly

VOTIVE RELIEF

Cat no. 56
Provenance: Sounion, near the temple of Athena, found in 1915
About 460 BC
Marble
48 (h) x 49.5 (w) cm
National Archaeological Museum, Athens, 3344

This is one of the finest Attic works of plastic art of the Severe style in the Classical period. It depicts a naked youth with his body turned three-quarters and his head shown in profile. In the upper left is the remains of the blue paint that once would have filled the background. The youth is placing a wreath on his head with his right hand. The wreath would have been made of metal and fixed in the holes that can be seen on the top of the head. The youth, who is depicted as a victorious athlete crowning himself, probably dedicated the relief in the sanctuary. Part of the top of the stele and roughly the bottom half are missing.

Nikolaos Kaltsas

Bibliography:

Ph Versakis. *AD 1916*, appendix, 77, fig. ι.

E Langlotz. *Frügriechische Buldhauerschülen*, Rome, 1967, 162, pl. 11.

R Lullies and M Hirmer. *Greek sculpture*, London, 1960, 70–1, pl. 96.

B S Ridgway. *The Severe style in Greek sculpture*, 1970, 49–50, fig. 70.

U Hausmann. *Griechische Weihreliefs*, Berlin, 1960, 23.

G Neumann. *Probleme der griechischen Weihreliefs*, Tübingen, 1979, 38, fig. 20b.

H Abramson. 'A hero shrine for Phrontis at Sounion', *California Studies in Classical Antiquity 12*, 1979, 4–5, pl. 1, fig. 2.

HEAD OF A YOUNG ATHLETE

Cat no. 57

Provenance: Athens

About 430 BC

Marble

20 (h) cm

National Archaeological Museum, Athens, no. 468

This head, from a hermaic stele or statue, has idealised features and depicts a wrestler or *pankratiast*, judging by the cauliflower ears. The ribbon he is wearing suggests that he was the victor in his event. The general workmanship and the quality of the sculpture point to an artist from the school of Pheidias' pupil, Agorakritos.

Nikolaos Kaltsas

Bibliography:

S Karousou. *National Archaeological Museum, sculpture collection*, 1968, p 53.

E Harrison. *The Athenian Agora XI*, 1965, 128ff., pl. 67c.

E Raftopoulou, in *Parthenon — Kongress Basel: Referate und Berichte*, E Berger, Mainz, 1984, 303ff., pls 50.1,2.

O Tzachou-Alexandri (ed.). *Mind and body: athletic contests in ancient Greece*, catalogue of the exhibition, Athens, 1989, p 334, no. 223 (V Machaira).

PANATHENAIC AMPHORA

Cat no. 58
By the Mastos Painter
Provenance: unknown
Second half of the 6th century BC
Clay
60 (h) x 17 (interior rim diam) x 19.8 (exterior rim diam) x 44 (belly diam) x 14 (base diam) cm
Nauplion Archaeological Museum, 1
Glymenopoulous collection

The neck of the amphora is adorned with floral decoration and palmettes. Added colours are purple and white. The anatomical details and the decorative motifs on the himatia worn by the figures are rendered by incision.

Side A depicts Athena *Promachos* facing left and holding a spear in her raised left hand. In her right hand she holds a shield on which the device is a triskelion. The goddess is flanked by Doric columns with cockerels standing on them. The left column has the inscription: ΤΟΝ ΑΘΕΝΕΘΕΝ ΑΘΛΟΝ (The prize from Athens).

Side B depicts a victory in an equestrian event. A naked youth on horseback, facing right and crowned with an olive branch, holds two more olive branches in his left hand. The horse is led by a bearded man wearing a himation. Another man touches the crown that has just been placed on the horse's head; in his right hand he holds a bunch of olive branches. A ribbon is fastened to the horse's rein. Behind the horse a beardless man wearing a himation holds out an olive branch with his right hand.

Katerina Barakari

Bibliography:

A Philadelpheus. *AD 18*, supplement 1918, pp 1–2, fig. 1.

J D Beazley. *The development of Attic black-figure*, Oxford, 1964, p 92, pl. 37.

J D Beazley. *Attic black-figure vase-painters*, reprint of 1956 edn, New York, 1978, p 260, no. 27.

DIMENSIONS AND ABBREVIATIONS

Dimensions of works have been given in centimetres (cm), height (h) or length (l) preceding width (w) preceding depth (d) preceding diameter (diam)

The following abbreviations have been used in the bibliographies for the catalogue entries:

Books

ABV = J D Beazley, *Attic black-figure vase painters*, Clarendon Press, Oxford,1956

ARV = J D Beazley, *Attic red-figure vase painters*, Clarendon Press, Oxford,1942

ARV² = J D Beazley, *Attic red-figure vase painters*, 2nd edn, Clarendon Press, Oxford,1963

CVA Athenes = *Corpus vasorum antiquorum, Grece, Athenes*

LIMC = *Lexicon iconographicum mythologiae classicae*

Journals

AD = *Archaiologikon Deltion*

AE = *Archaiologike Ephemeris*

AJA = *American Journal of Archaeology*

AM = *Mitteilungen des Deutschen Archaeologischen Instituts (DAI), Athenische Abteilung* = (bulletin of the German Archaeological Institute, Athens branch)

AM Beih. = (supplement to *AM*)

BCH = *Bulletin de Correspondance Hellénique*

BSA = *The Annual of the British School at Athens*

RM = *Mitteilungen des Deutschen Archaeologischen Instituts (DAI), Römische Abteilung*

'Vaulted stadium entry', a photograph taken at the end of the 1800s from within the sanctuary looking towards the stadium. Constructed around 190 BC, the arch was originally a complete tunnel under the embankment where spectators eagerly awaited their first view of the athletes.

F Adler, R Borrmann, W Dorpfeld, F Graeber, P Graef. *Die Baudenkmaler von Olympia*, Verlag Adolf Hakkert, Amsterdam, 1966 facsimile of 1897 original, Tafel I, plate T V.

GLOSSARY

Achilles
Greek warrior of Homer's *The Iliad*

Acropolis
Athenian citadel, dedicated to the goddess Athena, which includes the Parthenon

Aegina
Island in the Saronic Gulf

Aegis
Shoulder and chest armour

Akme
Peak of one's existence, around 18–20 years of age

Alabastron
A small perfume jar, sometimes made of alabaster, but more often of fine clay

Alkmene
Mother of Herakles

Altis
The sacred grove of Olympia

Alytarches
Steward in charge of running the games

Amphora
Two-handled jar used for storing and transporting liquids, especially wine

Amphoriskos
A small amphora

Angyle
Leather strap that assists in throwing a javelin

Antaios
Mythological giant, who was defeated by Herakles

Apobates
Athlete who would jump from a moving chariot, run beside it, and then attempt to jump back on

Apollo
Greek god of the sun, also of philosophy, music, and manly beauty, twin brother of Artemis

Archaic
Style of Greek art, 660–480 BC

Arete
Bravery, courage, personal excellence; later, moral virtue

Artemis
Greek earth goddess, symbolised by her hunting bow, twin sister of Apollo

Aryballos
Small perfume jar with a flat top, used to contain oil that was applied to an athlete's body before practice or competition

Astragal
Knucklebone

Athena
Goddess of wisdom, symbolised by an owl

Athena promachos
Athena 'In front of the battle line'

Athens
Democratic state of Greece, later became an empire

Attica
District of central Greece, which includes Athens

Bezel
Setting of a stone in a finger ring

Black-figure
Technique of vase painting, where figures are painted black against the natural red colour of the clay

Boeotia
District of central Greece

Bouleuterion
Meeting place for the Olympic council that supervised the day-to-day matters of running the sanctuary and games.

Bull-leaping
A contest in which young men and women leapt over the horns of a bull, possibly for fertility rituals or in honour of the gods.

Caduceus
Herald's staff, held by Hermes

Chiton
Linen shift, often girdled at the waist

Chlamys
Short woollen cloak

Classical
Style of Greek art, 480–323 BC

Colonnette
Small column symbolic of the palaestra

Consul
Roman civil and military magistrate

Corinth
Greek city-state in the north of the Peloponnese

Delphi
Site sacred to Apollo, famous for its oracle

Diadem
Small band fastened around the head, a symbol of victory

Diaulos
footrace twice as long as the *stadion*

Dioscuri
Castor and Polydeuces, twin sons of Zeus, who are reputed to be brilliant horsemen and so are associated with the sport

Diphroi Ocladiai
Small chair, like a stool

Dipylon Gate
Gateway through which the Sacred Road to Eleusis left Athens

Dodona
Site sacred to Zeus in the mountains of Epirus

Dolichos
Distance footrace

Drachma
Standard unit of Greek silver coinage

Elis
A district of the Peloponnese in Greece, of which Olympia is a part

Ephebos / Ephebe
Youth in his late teens (in Athens, aged 18 or 19)

Epistyle
The architrave or decorative band immediately above the columns of a temple

Exergue
Place on a coin beneath the ground-line of the design, commonly featuring an inscription

Geometric
Early style of Greek art (about 1025–700 BC)

Gymnasion/gymnasium
Literally 'naked place', exercise ground

Gymnos
Naked

Halteres
Hand-held weights, which helped propel the body further, used in long-jump

Helladic
Mycenaean period, contemporary with the Minoan period (about 3000–1100 BC)

Hellenistic
Style of Greek, 323–27 BC

Hellanodikai
Officials of the games

Hera
Goddess of marriage and women, wife of Zeus

Heraia
A festival held at Olympia for women that included a running race (five-sixths the length of the *stadion*). These were held between Olympiads.

Heraion
Temple of Hera

Herakles
Mythological Greek hero, on whose 12 labours the Olympic Games were based, and who personified the virtues of a great athlete

Hermes
Messenger god

Himantes
Leather thongs worn by a boxer to protect his hand and wrist

Himation
Long woollen cloak

Homer
Greek poet, who wrote the epics *The Iliad* and *The Odyssey*

Hoplite
Soldier

Hoplitodromos
'Running soldier', an athlete semi-clad in armour

Isthmian Games
Games held every two years at Isthmia, near Corinth, dedicated to Poseidon, and similar to those held in Olympia

Kalos
Good, beautiful, handsome, fair, high class

Kore
Girl, or a statue of one (in Archaic period)

Kotinos
Olive wreath of victory

Kouros
Youth, or a statue of one (in Archaic period)

Krater
Wide-mouthed bowl, made of either bronze or clay, for mixing wine with water

Kylix
Shallow drinking cup

Lekythos
Oil or perfume bottle with a thin neck, so that only small amounts could be poured at a time

Leto
Mother of Apollo and Artemis

Loutrophoros
Funerary vase

Minoan
Bronze Age civilisation of Crete

Mount Olympus
Mountain on the border of Thessaly and Macedonia, the mythological home of the gods.

Mycenaean
Bronze Age civilisation of Greece

Nemean Games
Panhellenic games held every two years at Nemea and dedicated to Zeus

Nereus
An old sea god, father of the Nereids, and often a spectator of Herakles' battles against Triton

Olympia
Site of the ancient Olympic games, in central Greece

Olympiad
Dates by which the Olympics were marked. The Greek calendar was divided into four years, each an Olympiad, which marked the year of the games at Olympia.

Oropos
Area on the north-eastern frontier between Attica and Boeotia

Palaestra
Part of the gymnasium, where wrestling and other sports were taught

Palmette
Fan-shaped decorative motif

Panathenaic Games
Athenian festival held every four years which incorporated games

Pankration
Competition, a combination of wrestling and boxing, of which the rules are unclear

Parthenon
Athenian temple dedicated to Athena Parthenos on the Acropolis

Parthenos
Virgin, maiden, unmarried girl

Patroklos
Greek warrior and friend of Achilles, mentioned in Homer's *Iliad* and for whom funerary games were held

Pelike
Two-handled jar, a heavier version of the amphora

Pentathlon
Five-event competition, which included wrestling, running, long jump, discus and javelin

Peplos
Sleeveless woollen shift, often girdled at the waist

Periodos
'Circuit' of games, referring to the four main games held in Greece: the Olympic, the Pythian, the Nemean and the Isthmian.

Piraeus
Harbour of Athens

Plataea
A city in south Boeotia

Plinth
Square base below a column or statue

Poseidon
Greek god of the sea and earthquakes

Procrustes
Mythical opponent of Theseus

Pylos
Mycenaean city of the western Peloponnese

Pythian Games
Games held every four years at Delphi, dedicated to Apollo, and similar to those in Olympia

Pyxis
Cylindrical box with a lid, used for cosmetics or jewellery

Red-figure
Technique of vase painting, where the figures remain the natural red colour of the clay, and the background is painted black around them

Rhyton
Ceremonial drinking vessel, often in the form of an animal

Samos
Island in the Aegean Sea off western Asia Minor

Santorini
Island state of the Aegean, part of an ancient volcano (also known as Thera)

Sarcophagus
Coffin

Sema
Sign, marker, monument

Siana cup
Type of kylix (cup) named after a cemetery in Rhodes where many have been found

Sirens
Mythological half-woman, half-bird creatures, known for their enchanting voices used to lure men to their deaths

Skyphos
Deep drinking cup with two handles

Sphinx
Mythological creature with a human head and the body of a lion

Spondophoroi
Heralds who travelled throughout Greece to announce the Sacred Truce associated with the games

Stadion
Sprint footrace (also known as *stade*)

Stele
Tall, narrow stone slab; some are grave markers, others bear inscriptions or religious scripture

Strigil
Long metal tool, used to scrape oil and dust off the body of an athlete after exercise

Strophia
Leather thongs that boxers wound around their hands, to protect them

Tanagra
City in Boeotia, central Greece

Thebes
City in Boeotia, central Greece

Themistoclean Walls
Defensive walls initially reconstructed by Themistocles against the Spartans, after the Persian Wars, 490–479 BC

Theseus
National hero of Athens and defeater of the Minotaur

Tiryns
Mycenaean city

Tondo
Circular central picture in a vase or bowl

Triskelion
Symbol of three curved branches radiating from centre

Triskeles
Symbol of three human legs radiating from centre

Triton
Sea demon or merman that appears in various Greek myths, including those of Herakles, and Jason and the Argonauts

Vapheio
Mycenaean site (*tholos* or beehive tomb) in Laconia on the Peloponnese

Votive
offering Inscriptions and reliefs dedicated to the gods, designed to be more lasting than a sacrificial offering

Zeus
King of the Greek gods, also god of thunder and patron of Olympia, whose temple is the focus of his sanctuary at Olympia.

Zeus Dodonaios
Epithet given to Zeus when at his sanctuary at Dodona

FURTHER READING

Ancient sources

Homer. *The Iliad*, tr. Richmond Lattimore, University of Chicago Press, Chicago, 1951.

Homer. *The Odyssey*, tr. Robert Fitzgerald, Doubleday, Garden City NY, 1961.

Pausanias. *Guide to Greece, vol. 2: southern Greece*, tr. Peter Levi, Penguin, London, 1979 (with revisions).

Pindar. *The odes of Pindas*, tr. C S Conway, J M Dent & Sons, London, 1972.

Plutarch. *Selected lives and essays*, tr. L R Loomis, Walter J Black Inc., Roslyn NY, 1951.

Greek art

Boardman, J. *Greek sculpture: the Archaic period*, Thames and Hudson, London, 1978.

Boardman, J. *Greek sculpture: the Classical period*, Thames and Hudson, London, 1985.

Burn, Lucilla. *The British Museum book of Greek and Roman art*, British Museum, London, 1991.

Carradice, Ian and Price, Martin. *Coinage in the Greek world*, Seaby, London, 1988.

Coldstream, J N. *Geometric Greece*, St Martin's Press, London and New York, 1977.

Dickinson, O. *The Aegean Bronze Age*, Cambridge University Press, Cambridge, 1994.

Kurke, Leslie. *Coins, bodies, games and gold: the politics of meaning in Archaic Greece*, Princeton University Press, Princeton NJ, 1999.

Pollitt, J J. *Art in the Hellenistic age*, Cambridge University Press, Cambridge, 1986.

Rasmussen, T and Spivey, N J (eds.). *Looking at Greek vases*, Cambridge University Press, Cambridge, 1991.

Richter, G M A. *The portraits of the Greeks*, 3 vols, London, 1965 (abridged and rev. by R R R Smith, Phaidon, Oxford, 1984).

Robertson, M. *The art of vase-painting in Classical Athens*, Cambridge University Press, Cambridge, 1992.

Schweitzer, B. *Greek Geometric art*, Phaidon, New York, 1971.

Shapiro, H A. *Art and cult under the tyrants in Athens*, P Von Zabern, Mainz, 1989.

Sparkes, B A. *Greek pottery: an introduction*, Manchester University Press, Manchester, 1991.

Sparkes, B A. *The red and the black: studies in Greek pottery*, Routledge, London, 1996.

Spivey, N J. *Understanding Greek sculpture*, Thames and Hudson, London, 1966.

Stewart, Andrew. *Art, desire and the body in ancient Greece*, Cambridge University Press, Cambridge, 1997.

Olympia and the Olympic Games

Crowther, N B. 'Athlete and state: qualifying for the Olympic Games in ancient Greece', *Journal of sport history*, 23, 1996, pp 34–43.

Douskou, Iris (ed.). *The Olympic Games in ancient Greece*, Ekdotike Athenon, Athens, 1982.

Drees, L. *Olympia: gods, artists and athletes*, English tr., Pall Mall Press, London, 1968.

Harris, H A. *Greek athletes and athletics*, Hutchison, London 1964 and Indiana University Press, Bloomington IN, 1966.

Olivova, Vera. *Sports and games in the ancient world*, Orbis, London, 1984.

Raschke, W J (ed.). *The archaeology of the Olympics: the Olympics and other festivals in antiquity*, University of Wisconsin Press, Madison WI, 1988.

Spathari, E. *The Olympic spirit*, Adams Editions, Athens, 1992.

Swaddling, J. *The ancient Olympic Games*, British Museum, London, 1999.

Sweet, W. *Sport and recreation in ancient Greece*, Oxford University Press, Oxford, 1987.

Tzachou-Alexandri, O (ed.). *Mind and body: athletic contests in ancient Greece*, catalogue of the exhibition, Ministry of Culture and the National Hellenic Committee, (ICOM), Athens, 1989.

Historical, social and archaeological background

Blundell, S. *Women in ancient Greece*, Harvard University Press, Cambridge MA, 1995

Bremmer, Jan N. *Greek religion*, Oxford University Press, Oxford, 1994.

Burker, W. *Greek religion*, Blackwell, Oxford and Cambridge MA, 1985.

Gantz, T. *Early Greek myths: a guide to literary and artistic sources*, 2 vols, Johns Hopkins University Press, Baltimore MD, 1993.

Kurtz, D C and Boardman, J. *Greek burial customs*, Thames and Hudson, London, 1971.

Price, Simon. *Religions of the ancient Greeks*, Cambridge University Press, Cambridge, 1999.

Webster, T B L. *Life in Classical Athens*, Batsford, London, 1969.

ABOUT AUTHORS

THE ESSAYS

Terence Measham, AM FRSA

During his period as director of the Powerhouse Museum (1988–99), Terence Measham completed more than three decades of writing books, journal articles and reviews. In London, where his interest in Greek art began, he studied at the Courtauld Institute of Art, and worked at the Tate Gallery for ten years. In the course of planning the exhibition and publication *1000 years of the Olympic Games: treasures of ancient Greece,* Measham visited Athens five times for discussions with the Greek Ministry of Culture. The themes and objects for the exhibition are the fruit of that collaboration.

Elisabeth Spathari

Elisabeth Spathari is a curator of antiquities and has been the director of the 4th Ephorate of Prehistoric and Classical Antiquities in Nauplion, Greece, since 1997. She studied archaeology at the Department of Philosophy at the National Capodistrian University in Athens and conducted postgraduate studies in ancient architecture and town planning at the Sorbonne in Paris. Since 1963 she has worked at the Archaeological Service and since 1985 she has been involved with the archaeological exhibitions of the Ministry of Culture in Greece and elsewhere. In 1989 she became a member of the team in charge of the preparation of the file for the candidature of Athens for the Golden Olympiad (1996).

As well as various articles and reviews, she has published the following monographs: *The Olympic spirit,* Adams Editions, Athens, 1992; *Sailing in time: the ship in Greek art,* Capon Editions, Athens, 1995; and *The ancient Greek theatres,* Pl. Maximos, Athens, 1998.

Paul Donnelly

Paul Donnelly is a curator of decorative arts and design at the Powerhouse Museum. A graduate of archaeology at the University of Sydney, he also has an MA in applied history. He is a regular participant on the archaeological expedition to Pella in Jordan, and is currently enrolled in a doctorate focussing on ceramics of the Middle Bronze Age period in the eastern Mediterranean. He is curator of *1000 years of the Olympic Games: treasures of ancient Greece.* As well as writing journal articles on both ancient and modern topics, he has contributed to a number of publications including *Australian gold and silver 1851–1900* (Powerhouse Publishing, Sydney, 1995) and *Convict love tokens* (Wakefield Press, Adelaide, 1998).

THE WORKS

Xenia Arapoyianni studied at the National Capodistrian University of Athens. She worked for many years as an archaeologist in Attica and conducted important excavations. Since 1980 she has been head of the 7th Ephorate of Prehistoric and Classical Antiquities (Elis, Messenia and Zakynthos) and director of the Olympia Museum. She has published many articles in archaeological journals and encyclopedias, and has recently completed her PhD.

Eleni Banou graduated from the National Capodistrian University of Athens in 1980 and completed a doctorate on 'Pottery groups from the west side of area A at Pseira, Crete' at the University of Pennsylvania, USA in1992. She joined the Archaeological Service in 1985 and has worked in the 25th and 13th Ephorates of Prehistoric and Classical Antiquities. She has been published in academic journals on the subject of Minoan civilisation. Since 1995 she has been co-director of the excavation of the Minoan harbour settlement at Rethymnon.

Katerina Barakari graduated in 1973, and received her postgraduate degree in Classical archaeology in 1994, from the National Capodistrian University of Athens. She works in the 4th Ephorate of Prehistoric and Classical Antiquities, Nauplia, and has conducted many excavations. Her articles and studies have been published in journals and the proceedings of international conferences relating to the architecture and topography of the Archaic and Classical periods.

Pat Boland OAM, ED is honorary numismatist at the Powerhouse Museum, Sydney. He was curator of numismatics at the museum from 1961 — 88 when the numismatic collection doubled to over 30 000 items. In 1977 he was awarded a Churchill Fellowship for numismatic research. His significant contribution has been recognised by being the only staff member of the museum ever to be honoured as Life Fellow — the museum's highest award and one of only five ever made.

Anastasia Gadolou is a curator of antiquities and is currently working in the Department of Educational Programs of the Greek Ministry of Culture. She has worked for the Greek Archaeological Service since 1994 in the 6th and 9th Ephorates of Prehistoric and Classical Antiquities (Patras and Thebes respectively). She completed a postgraduate degree in landscape studies at Leicester University, England and received a PhD (2000) at the National Capodistrian University of Athens.

Nikolaos Kaltsas is a curator of antiquities and is head of the sculpture collection at the National Archaeological Museum. He completed his PhD in 1985 at the Aristotelian University of Thessaloniki. He has been a research associate at CNRS in Paris; a curator at Thessaloniki and the Olympia Museum; and head of the Museums Department, Ministry of Culture. He has participated in many excavations and organising committees for exhibitions in Greece and overseas; and his publications include *Decorated architectural terracottas from Macedonia,* 1988 and *Akanthos: the excavations in the cemetery in 1979,* 1998.

Vasiliki Orphanou studied archaeology and German philology at the Universities of Athens and Tübingen (MA). Since 1986 she has worked in the Greek Archaeological Service and has conducted archaeological excavations in Epiros (Arta), Corinth and Athens. She is now a curator in the 3rd Ephorate of Prehistoric and Classical Antiquities. Her major area of interest is ancient Greek religion.

Rosa Proskynitopoulou is a curator of antiquities and has been head of the bronze collection of the National Archaeological Museum, Athens since 1990. She studied history and archaeology at the National Capodistrian University of Athens, and has worked in the Greek Archaeological Service since 1974 (including Olympia, Elis and Epidauros). She has published many articles on archaeology and has contributed to the design and writing of catalogues for exhibitions organised by the Greek Ministry of Culture.

Alkestis Spetsieri-Choremi is director of the 1st Ephorate of Classical Antiquities (Acropolis, Athens). She is a graduate of and holds a PhD from the National Capodistrian University of Athens. She is a member of the Archaeological Society of Athens and the German Archaeological Institute. She has excavated at various archaeological sites in Greece and has published the results as well as articles in academic journals, and has participated in congresses in Greece, Europe and the USA.

Elisabeth Stassinopoulou-Kakarouga is a curator of antiquities in the vase collection of the National Archaeological Museum, Athens, and has worked with the Greek Archaeological Service since 1974. She studied at the National Capodistrian University of Athens and has conducted excavations in Boeotia. At NAM she has worked on exhibitions of the vase and Stathatos collections, and temporary exhibitions held in Greece and abroad.

Pavlos Triandaphyllidis studied archaeology at Ioannina University, after which he completed a doctorate in Classical archaeology on the glassware of Minoan Amorgos. He is currently working in the 22nd Ephorate of Prehistoric and Classical Antiquities and studying the glassware of Rhodes with a scholarship from Harvard University. His publications include *Rhodian glassware I: the hot-formed transparent luxury vessels of the classical and early Hellenistic period* (Ministry of the Aegean, Athens, 2000).

Maria Viglaki is a curator of antiquities in the 21st Ephorate of Prehistoric and Classical Antiquities. She is a graduate of the National Capodistrian University of Athens. She has conducted excavations on Paros and Delos and is in charge of the excavation of the Geometric Cemetery on Samos. She is co-author of the book *Samos: the Sanctuary of Hera,* published as part of the MELINA educational program.

Maria Vlassopoulou-Karydi has been a curator of the prehistoric collection of the National Archaeological Museum, Athens since 1974. She studied and completed a postgraduate degree in Mycenaean seats and seated figurines at the National Capodistrian University of Athens. Her publications include *Clay Mycenaean models of seats and seated figurines,* 1998; *Ivory mirror handles in the Mycenaean collection of the National Archaeological Museum of Athens* (in press); and *The origin and spread of Arcadians in antiquity* (in press).

Mary Zaphiropoulou is a curator of antiquities in the bronze collection of the National Archaeological Museum, Athens. She is a graduate of the National Capodistrian University of Athens and also holds a degree in English literature from the same university. She has an MA in museum studies from Leicester University and has worked at the British, Birmingham and Leicestershire museums. Since 1973 she has worked in the Greek Archaeological Service and has contributed to various publications.

ABOUT THE POWERHOUSE MUSEUM

The Powerhouse Museum is Australia's largest and most popular museum. Established in 1880, it is a museum of decorative arts, design, science, technology and social history with a collection that encompasses Australian and international, historical and contemporary material culture. In 1988 the museum moved into new premises, a refurbished power station.

The mission of the Powerhouse Museum is to inspire diverse audiences by using the collection and scholarship to provide informative and innovative exhibitions, programs and services. The Powerhouse Museum has a reputation for quality and excellence in collecting, preserving and presenting aspects of world cultures for present and future generations.

The Powerhouse Museum's exhibitions are renowned for innovative interactive exhibits and the use of new technologies. For *1000 years of the Olympic Games: treasure of ancient Greece*, the museum has used a number of new virtual-reality technologies to enrich the exhibition.

In partnership with the University of Melbourne, the museum has created a full virtual reconstruction of ancient Olympia. The recreation of the ancient Olympic precinct, including temples adorned with marble sculpture, was accomplished through extensive research into ancient Greek architecture using archaeological reports and historic sources. Visitors are transported through time to about 200 BC to explore this environment in three dimensions.

A 3D model of the large bronze statue of Zeus from Artemision, currently on display in the National Archaeological Museum in Athens, is also included in the exhibition. A team of experts travelled from Australia to capture the object in high resolution using a laser scanner and digital photography. This highly complex dataset has been translated into an 'immersive' experience that conveys the great presence of the statue using a new imaging technique developed at the Australian National University, Canberra.

The exhibition is complemented by an extensive website (http://www.phm.gov.au/ancient_greek_olympics/) that gives access to the 3D models and a wealth of information and photography related to objects in the exhibition. The website provides supplementary educational material and resources for exploring the glory of ancient Olympia. All these digital components were made possible by the generous support of Intel Semiconductor Ltd (http://www.intel.com.au)